HMS Illustrious

After further repairs at Alexandria, the Illustrious *sailed for the United States, where she was restored and made fit for service again.*

FORTUNES OF WAR

HMS Illustrious

KENNETH POOLMAN

CERBERUS

First published by William Kimber & Co Limited, in 1955.

PUBLISHED IN THE UNITED KINGDOM BY;
Cerberus Publishing Limited
22A Osprey Court
Hawkfield Business Park
Bristol
BS14 0BB
UK
e-mail: cerberusbooks@aol.com
www.cerberus-publishing.com

© Cerberus Publishing Ltd 2004

British Library Cataloguing in Publication Data.
A catalogue record for this book is available from the British Library.

ISBN 1 84145 048 0

PRINTED AND BOUND IN ENGLAND.

Contents

Acknowledgements

I owe a great debt of gratitude to all the people who have helped me to write this book.

Above all I want to thank Lieutenant Commander (A) Norman Hanson, DSC, RNVR, for all the time and enthusiasm which he has spent in helping to prepare this story of the ship he loved and served so well.

I owe my deepest thanks also to the Department of the Chief of Naval Information at the Admiralty, particularly Mr Reg Holmes, and to many former officers and men of HMS *Illustrious*, especially Admiral Sir Denis Boyd, KCB, CBE, DSC, Admiral Sir A Lumley St G Lyster, KCB, CVO, CBE, DSO, Commodore C L O Evans, CBE, DSO, DSC, Lieutenant W W Banham, Dr R Efflson, Commander G R M Going, DSO, OBE, Captain G S Tuck, Captain J I Robertson, CBB, Captain K Williamson, DSO, Captain J de P Jago, Commander J W Hale, DSO, Captain M E Butler-Bowdon, OBE, Captain A H Wallis, CBB, and Captain H R B Janvrin, DSC, all of whom gave me very great help in collecting material, as did the Public Information Office of the United States Navy, the Imperial War Museum and the builders of *Illustrious*, Messrs. Vickers Armstrongs. I am also grateful to Hugh Popham for permission to quote from his poem, 'Against the Lightning. A Poem from an Aircraft Carrier', published by Messrs. John Lane.

To these and all the others who were kind enough to write or talk to me about *Illustrious* I wish to convey my sincerest thanks and the hope that they may enjoy the result.

CHAPTER ONE

In The Beginning...

She looked worse than a hull when Bill Bantam saw her first, on a cold November day in 1938. She wasn't called *Illustrious* 'men – just another job number in Vickers-Armstrongs' Shipbuilding Works, Barrow-in-Furness.

When he first wandered into me main yards he could see no sign of any warship under construction, only a wilderness of spars and derricks, tall cranes and slipways that sttcred like great tramlinia down into the dirty green water of the Walney Channel. On one at these tramlines lay a long carcase, keel, ribs and what looked like a second deck all brown with rust. It looked like a great fish picked clean and lying on a greasy plate. This was No. 732.

She was his ship and he had come to help build her. The right of her bare and rusty bones stretched out in number-two berth did not worry him unduly. Bill was an old hand and had stood by ships before. He knew how a fine ship oould grow out of cold metal, provided you loved her and worked hard for her.

He had toyed the old *Grimsby* when he had stood by her all those years ago. She had been new too, the first of her line like No. 732, a fine sloop, a minelayer and a minesweeper. She had been a bit of a facer for a while to a brand-new Warrant Gunner, for he had had to learn all about mines and their ways while the shop was leading in Devonport dockyard. But he had got that problem straightened out in due course, drawing on the same stubborn drive and 'don't let anything master you' spirit mat had beaten the handicap of an elementary school education and passed the stiff examinations that made him an officer.

Here was No. 732, then, and another problem for her new Gunner – an aircraft-carrier this time, the capital ship of the future the Fleet Air Arm boys said, a great ship of 28,000 tons, with all kinds of new armament to be fitted and learned, me first of a new design, with no forerunner to go by.

She was a new venture for her builders, too. No. 732 and her sister, 735, which lay building near her, were the first aircraft-carriers Vickers, Barrow, had ever built. The film had a long and distinguished history and had launched liners, cargo vessels and warships in a steady stream since 1873. Oddly enough, they had tended to specialise, as far as warship construction went in submarines. In fact they had launched the very first 'submarine boat' built for the Royal Navy in 1901, and for many years afterwards had built all British submarines. Now a new phase of specialised construction was to begin for this great and famous shipbuilding firm. From planning and building vessels that went down into the green and silent deeps to strike with torpedoes, they developed their fine skill and expertise to fashion ships whose striking power went upwards into the sky from great flat steeel decks like floating airfields and attacked the enemy with torpedo and bomb from the opposite element.

When Bill and others like him came to Barrow to make this weird new, flat-topped contraption ship-shape, they brought the greatness of the old Royal Navy with them, a genius of seamanship and dash, the old pride of a fleet that had always held the sea, and kept station, canvas and steam, frigate, ship-of-the-line and dreadnought, for centuries of grey weather, long before the aeroplane set its brittle wings against the wind.

He didn't know much about *Illustrious*, except that she was to be the last word in carriers and, by the look of things, was going to be badly needed at sea in the not too distant future. It was only a few weeks after Munich, and already the suspicion was growing that the agreement which Hitler, Mussolini and Mr Chamberlain had signed was just another scrap of diplomatic flimsy to be blown in the next hot blast of totalitarian aggression.

It was more than a suspicion in Service circles. About this time the Commander-in-Chief, Mediterranean, Admiral Sir Dudley Pound, sent for Captain A Lumley St G Lyster, commanding the aircraft-carrier *Glorious* in the Mediterranean Fleet, and asked him bluntly:

'Can you send a torpedo attack against me Italian Fleet on the night war breaks out?'

'Yes,' said Lyster, 'I can.'

He was promising something which had never been done before, a thing which many senior naval officers said was impossible – a major attack by torpedo bombers against an enemy battle fleet. Most people realised that carrier-borne aeroplanes were here to stay, but very few thought that they could do alone what battleships had always done. A lucky torpedo might slow an enemy down for the big guns of the Fleet to finish off, but for aircraft to do the whole job was asking too much.

But this job aircraft would have to tackle alone. The Italian Fleet would almost certainly be lying in harbour, where our guns could not reach them. It would be a test, and a severe one, for the new blanch.

Could they do it? 'No,' said die-hard gunners, 'they will be shot down before they can launch their torpedoes.'

Lyster himself was a gunnery expert and knew better than, most what his attacking torpedo bombers would have to face from anti-aircraft fire. He feared for the lives of his young men if attack were ever made, but he believed they could do it.

He had trained them to do it. Such an attack would have to be made under cover of darkness, and Lyster and his Commander (Air), Guy Willoughby, had already made sure that their aircrews were as at home in the air at night as they were by day. They were the cream of naval aviation, these men, there were no better anywhere in me world, and they were ready.

All the aircraft-carriers of the Royal Navy were ready. The trouble was that they were getting on in years and there were only five of them. *Furious*, *Glorious* and *Courageous*, carriers with a reasonably large number of aircraft apiece, were conversions from the 'large light cruisers' originally built in the Great War by Lord Fisher for his abortive 'Baltic Armada'. And they were unarmoured. *Eagle*, converted on the stocks from a battleship, carried only eighteen torpedo bombers, and *Hermes*, the only one designed and built from the start as a carrier, only nine. New carriers were building or planned but they were a long way off completion.

This was not me fault of the Admiralty. They had held steady in a situation made uncertain and frustrating to a degree by wishful disarmament and a parsimonious Treasury, as well as by lack of reliable knowledge of the real power of aeroplanes against warships. The Admiralty had done the best it could, effecting a difficult compromise between all the disturbing factors which beset naval policy in me first two decades after the Great War. British naval aviation was, perhaps, not quite so go-ahead as Japanese or American, but we were not far behind, and what equipment we did have was always maintained at first-rate efficiency.

The Great War had ended without proving anything more than the worth of aircraft, weather permitting, to search out me enemy fleet and to spot for me big guns, and this view prevailed in the Navy until the early thirties. Aeroplanes would assist warships but would not in any way substitute for guns either in attack or defence.

The Fleet Air Arm of the Royal Navy, formed in 1924, the force entrusted with this minor task, was kept as a minor branch. The old Royal Naval Air Service, a highly skilled and enthusiastic band of brothers, had been, absorbed into me new Royal Air Force on its formation in 1918, and the men and machines of the Fleet Air Arm were part of the Royal Air Force, with the exception of observers and a proportion of pilots, who were seconded from the Navy. Co-operation between RAF and Royal Navy afloat was cordial, but the division of control by which an arm of the Fleet was a mere part of Coastal Area, RAF, was thoroughly bad for naval flying.

The Fleet Air Arm came off very much second best in equipment. Their machines were always either far below the performance of the RAF aircraft of the time, or far too few in number. Hardly anyone imagined then that the Fleet Air Arm would ever have to face land-based fighters and bombers or that fast-performance machines could ever be made to land on a carrier's deck. Very often, too, the poor sister was given Royal Air Force cast-offs in the shape of men the shore squadrons were glad to get rid of, although many of the Air Force pilot serving with the Fleet were splendid fliers and keen enthusiasts for carrier work.

Then, in 1931, Rear-Admiral R G Henderson, a Fleet Air Arm enthusiast, was appointed Rear-Admiral, Aircraft Carriers, and immediately set about the task of raising the Cinderella of the Navy to her proper status. Things began to improve, although the fact that as few as eighteen machines were added to the strength of the Fleet Air Arm between 1929 and 1932 showed plainly the frustrating slowness of the process. Britain was now disarming and there were few felt to worry about the future of the air branch of the Navy. Fortunately for us there were some, and these were as pure as gold.

Nor was disarmament the only obstacle. Opinion was hopelessly divided on the question of aircraft versus warship.

Hot-headed bomber boffins said that aircraft could sink any warship afloat, that the day of the Navy was gone. Retired admirals angrily dismissed the bomber as a gadfly which either the weather or naval guns would make short work of.

Truth lay somewhere in between. Exactly what the answer was no one knew. However, it seemed only common sense that there would be occasions in any war of the future when aircraft could be made effective at sea, particularly against an enemy battle fleet with a superior turn of speed to our own, provided the aircraft themselves could be brought within striking distance of the enemy. It seemed only common sense, too, that only the aircraft-carrier could bring these advantages into operation over those areas of ocean which land-based bombers had insufficient fuel capacity to reach and search efficiently and still carry enough bombs or torpedoes to attack effectively. As to the tactical problems of ship versus aeroplane, time atone could tell whether anti-aircraft guns and carrier-borne fighters were adequate to defend the Fleet. Meanwhile it was quite obvious that an orthodox fleet would still be necessary.

This was the Admiralty's view, and the result could be seen in the imaginative use of the Navy's small carrier force in the years of co-operation with the RAF. During this time high-level, dive-bombing and torpedo attacks, and night navigation and attack, were practised thoroughly by RAF and naval airmen who had much to teach each other in flying technique and torpedo warfare respectively, as well as the actual techniques of rapid and efficient landing on and flying off a carrier's deck. Foremost in all this was the *Glorious*, with Lumley Lyster's young men making free of the skies above Mussolini's 'Italian lake'.

But still the Fleet Air Arm lagged far behind the rest of the RAF in equipment. Still the Royal Navy, whose ships remained the bedrock of the nation's defence, lacked its own air branch. And the signs of war were multiplying every day. The shadow of Nazi and Fascist bombers fell over Spain and Abyssinia. The Navy was alerted. Fleet Air Arm squadrons sunning themselves ashore at Hal Far, in Malta, scrambled aboard *Glorious* for what turned out to be, to their intense chagrin, a false alarm.

The signs, in fact, had become too obvious to ignore. Britain at long last was rearming.

1936 was me year in which the struggling Fleet Air Arm first saw a gleam appear in the darkness that had hidden their best efforts so far. The first sign of the change was the commencement of work on a new aircraft-carrier to be given the proud name of *Ark Royal*, a fine new ship of space and light and speed built to carry sixty aircraft, bigger than the new *Enterprise* and *Yorktown*, then building for the United States Navy, and the Japanese *Chitose*, launched from a Kure yard on November 29th.

Among aircraft-carriers the *Ark Royal* was to be, as the First Lord of the Admiralty, Sir Samuel Hoare, said after her launching, 'the most up to date in the world'. And she was not alone. New ships provided for in the 1936 programme of construction included two more big carriers, besides two battleships, seven cruisers, seventeen destroyers and seven submarines. Our shipyards began to stir.

Naval Bstimates for 1937 allowed for an eapcnditure of £105,065,000, an increase of £23,776,000 over 1936. The main increase was in the provision for new construction. British tax-payers were asked to spend £14,033,215 on new ships for their protection. For their money they would get three more new battleships, two more new aircraft-carriers, seven cruisers, sixteen destroyers, seven submarines, and a number of minesweeepers and escort and patrol vessels.

This meant that, when work finally commenced on the latest two, there would be four new carriers under construction for the Navy. To help fill their hangars an increase of £516,500 was allowed for in the Navy Estimates to pay for new aircraft. Contracts for the new ships were placed with unprecedented speed.

Then, in the summer of this dramatic year, came an even greater boost to the morals of naval aviation, an event long desired by all progressive naval officers. The Prime Minister, Mr Neville Chamberlain, announced in the House of Commons that the Fleet Air Arm was to be handed over to the Navy. Agitation to this end had been going on for some time both inside and outside Service circles and now at last the Government had seen the light. Mr Chamberlain said,

'The proposals which the Government have had under their consideration refer to two classes of aircraft. The first class includes all aircraft borne in ships of the Royal Navy. These are known as the Fleet Air Arm. They are under the operational control of the Admiralty, but as part of the Royal Air Force they are under the administrative control of the Air Ministry.

'The second class includes shore-based aircraft employed in co-operation with naval forces. These are under the operational as well as the administrative control of the Air Ministry... The Government have decided that in the case of the second class, namely, shore-based aircraft, which term includes flying boats, there shall be no alteration in the present systems.

'In the case of the Fleet Air Arm, the Government consider that these ship-borne aircraft should be placed under the administrative control of the Admiralty.'

The Navy had got its air branch back. All RAF flying and maintenance personnel would go back to their own Service – and the Navy would have to fill their places, as well as man and equip the new carriers when they came into service and establish a chain of naval air stations. It was a tall order, and they were to have two years to complete the change-over.

The Admiralty set about me task with vigour. A 'Fifth Sea Lord and Chief of Navel Air Services' was added to the Board of Admiralty, and the various departments necessary to handle naval air material and personnel were created. The entry of short-service officers for flying duties and the training of ratings as pilots, both measures previously opposed by the Admiralty, were started early in 1938, and the Royal Naval Volunteer Reserve Air Branch was formed in the autumn of the same year.

And now *Ark Royal* was commissioned, the first carrier of the new Fleet Air Arm, and Captain Power took her to sea, the symbol of a great renaissance of naval strength and modern striking force.

She set a new fashion in carriers, with better flight-deck arrangements, a vastly unproved system for aircraft stowage and maintenance and for stores and greater comfort for her ship's company. But she was still weakly protected and had no armour to speak of. Six more new ships were to remedy this, ships which really formed a class of their own.

The first of this class was No. 732, building at Vickers-Armstrongs, Barrow.

She was ordered on January 13th, 1937. The Admiralty design for the ship went to the firm's Naval Architect Department, where the general arrangement of the ship and such aspects of the design as the hydrostatics – the arrangement of the tanks which were to give the ship stability – and the quantities of metals needed were checked and assessed. Once these details had been agreed with the Admiralty, each department of the firm could get down to its particular share in the new carrier's birth. The Designing Office prepared 'offsets' or figures correctly describing in detail the lines of the ship about her hull, and passed them to, the Ship Drawing Office and to the Loft, where full-scale plans were prepared. The Drawing Office worked up the general arrangement drawings – piping drawings, ventilators, heaters, all the store-rooms, magazines, bomb rooms, messing and sleeping spaces, rigging and boats, and all the hangar and aircraft arrangements – everything, in short, contained within the hull. When they had prepared them all, they had two thousand five hundred separate plans marked 'No. 732' in the office. Not included in this figure were all the mechanical drawings, which were prepared elsewhere by the technical departments concerned.

When the Loft had completed full-scale drawings on its enormous floors, the elegant curves of this new lady of the seas were transferred to the plate shops, where they became real and actual at last. This was where the shipyard manager looking after 732, Mr Nicholson, and his shipyard foreman, Mr Parnell, came into the picture. They had to build this ship, the first aircraft-carrier their yard had ever tackled.

Her keel was laid on April 27th, 1937, and her graceful hull slowly began to take shape on the sloping berth under the steel vultures of the cranes. After the flat keel came the plates of the outer bottom, then the vertical keel and the inner bottom, and then, a significant stage, her first main watertight bulkheads. She sprang up like a tree out of the ground, growing side panels of steel, shell plating, pillars and girders, divisional bulkheads, bomb rooms, hollow machinery spaces, and finally the flat firmness of her decks, when at last it began to look as if men were meant to walk about in her on their feet and not swing about on her metal beams like monkeys.

On top of all this apparent jumble of steel boxes crammed together inside her sloping, slender sides, they put the last, and biggest box of all, the thing that made sense out of this odd-looking ship-shape – her hangar. Unlike the *Ark*, unlike her American and Japanese sisters, in this ship it was to be an armoured box, four and a half inches thick at the sides, with a three-inch-thick lid and armoured doors at each end.

To incorporate all this unusual top weight in a warship, and still preserve her stability, was a great achievement on the part of Mr W A D Fortes, the Admiralty naval architect concerned, and his department. They did it by making the, box of the hangar a firm and integral part of the strength structure of the whole ship. Basically, a ship is a great girder drawn in at both ends, the girder structure giving her the strength to fight the seas. In a liner there is always one main deck, fairly low down in the ship, which forms the top surface of this girder and is called the 'strength deck' of the ship. All the ship's structure above this deck, promenade deck, boat deck, etc, if a comparatively flimsy structure. It was the same with the new camera which the Americans were building. In an American carrier the hangar deck, the 'floor' of the hangar, was the strength deck. Above this was built a light hangar with a thin flight deck topped with wooden planking 'open' along the sides by the use of sliding doors and shutters, and thus easy of access.

The principle built into tbe new British carriers was very different. In 732 her armoured flight deck was her strength deck. The arrangement which this imposed upon the rest of the shay meant less room for aircraft than in the American ships and there was no comparable access through the sides of such a solid structure. But it was hoped that the armour plate would deny access to other things than stores or planes – to five-hundred-pound bombs, in fact. This was the idea behind 732's 'closed-hangar', as it was called.

It was a brilliant idea but it gave the shipyard foreman some bad moments. The great four-and-a-half-inch-thick bulkheads forming the sides of the hangar made of specially treated concreted armour plate had been pre-fabricatied elsewhere and arrived as huge unwieldy slabs, far too tough to cut, which had to be placed into exact positions. It proved impossible to lift them into postion upright, so, one by one, they were laid flat on the hanger deck and levered up into place. Bridging over them huge beams four feet deep, were laid, ready to receive the weight of the three-inch armoured flight deck. The plates of flight deck were not all riveted down at once, a long stretch of plating being left only loosely bolted so that this section could be removed again when the ship's main machinery was put in after launching.

Halfway through all this striving and planning, this toiling and sweating, that was slowly and painstakingly building a great ship out of steel and paper, the first men of her future ship's company came to Barrrow.

Going north in the train, Bill Banham thought to himself, 'You're a lucky bastard to get this appointment, only a thin-ring gunner – usually goes to a; two-ringer, a big thing like this, big new carrier. *Make the most of it!'*

He arrived at Barrow in November 1938 and went straight to his digs in Ocean Road, Walney Island, where Mr and Mrs Thompson made him immediately at home. Mrs Thompson soon found her way to his heart, when she produced a baked pie of tomatoes, macaroni and cheese. Next day, much fortified, he reported to the works manager's office at Vickers-Armstrongs and was introduced to the men he would be working with during the months to come. He was given an office – and his lunch and a good 'nip' free from then on, a favour which he was still matelot enough to appreciate. He visited all the various shps and departments where the ship lived only on paper or in strange distorted steel bits and pieces.

He was her armaments officer, and the guns, the magazines and bomb rooms were his special target. The new carrier's main gun power was to consist of new pattern 4.5-inch combined high- and low-angle gun and a new type of eight-barrel multiple two-pounder pom-pom anti-aircraft weapon of high velocity. No one knew anything about these guns and less than nothing as to what bombs the ship would carry within her. They were all 'makee learns'.

Each day was filled with the clangour of the yard, the shattering jammer of tools on metal, with shouting and sweating and frantic attempts to think straight and NOISE, NOISE, NOISE, until the head ached and the brain throbbed. But amidst this bedlam the blueprints began to stand up in tall and curved reality as the hull, the spaces, the offices and gun emplacements came into being within that rust-covered case of ribs and plating. Two decks became three, then four, then five, then six. She was taking shape all right now, though she still looked a bunch of bastards, thought Bill. He was beginning to get quite fond of the great gawky female and secretly enjoyed the heart-breaking process of turning her into a woman. With a yacht or a sloop or an MTB it was like breathing life into a baby; with a big ship it was usually more like building a great house, an ark, to shelter in against the weather and the wrath of man.

But here these similes did not fit. Here they were forging a ship-size statue out at steel and sculpting it with flame and hammer – not a classical beauty, like a slim cruiser or a noble battleship, but a bizarre and romantic one, not a lady, perhaps, but a fast and beautiful bitch. That's what all this clangour and frantic bustle meant. This was a famous beauty putting on her war-paint. Even now a thousand men waited hand, foot, and finger upon her. Even now she had the power to make men sweat and swear and some of them despair and go prematurely grey... men like Nicholson and Parnell and Bill Banham who had to look after her and sponsor her and launch her into the society of the seas.

There was some delay in fitting the flight deck. Its sections had been sub-contracted elsewhere and were late in arriving at Barrow. When they did arrive there was further delay in cutting out the two rectangular holes fore and aft where the aircraft lifts for carrying aircraft to and from the hangar below would fit flush with the flight deck. No one at that stage knew what aircraft the ship would carry, as the procurement of aeroplanes for the new Fleet Air Arm was in a very undecided and unsatisfactory state. It was no good cutting through the three-inch armour only to find that the holes were the wrong size.

Once a week Bill Banham would visit Gunnery Drawing Office, where blueprints were being prepared for Admiralty approval. These were shown to him for his comments and he suggested any alterations or amendments he thought necessary in the light of his long experience as a gunner. The prints were then taken to the Admiralty by a liaison officer and in a week or two it would be known whether they were approved or not.

One of the first things Bill did was to invent a new type of magazine keyboard for the ship. There were fifty-two compartments inside the hull, built to contain explosives of one kind or another. These compartments were controlled by literally hundreds of keys, making the old type of magazine keyboard useless. The keys gave access through all the numerous hatches and doors necessary to the watertight integrity of the ship. If the keyboard was not organised properly you might easily find yourself at the bottom of the ship without that last important key, and a long way to go back to the keyboard. So Bill planned a keyboard which was coloured according to types of explosives and interconnected by thin coloured lines from key to key. When it was finished the whole thing looked like a map of the London tubes. But it worked, and all ships after this had the same type of keyboard.

One by one other officers representing other departments in the ship were coming to Barrow and standing by, to carry out similar work to Bill's. There were delays, of course, frustrating and infuriating. Drawings awaiting approval at the Admiralty sometimes loafed there for months. Every week when the liaison officer went to the Admiralty he would take with him, besides new blueprints, reminders of previous drawings which were still outstanding and were holding up completion. One construction shop waited five months to make about a hundred five-gallon fresh-water tanks to be placed in various 'action' positions in the ship. Every week with gloomy regularity the liaison officer reported, 'No, they haven't settled the design yet.' Finally the builders and the Navy men on the spot could wait no longer. A type of tank was agreed upon, the required number were made and fixed in position throughout the ship. Some weeks late Admiralty-approved drawings for a set of tanks totally unsuitable for the new ship and based on tanks fitted in earlier and older vessels arrived. There were other, similar cases.

'What do you reckon's the reason for these blessed hold-ups?' asked Bill one day, when he was chatting to one of the Drawing Office officials.

'Well, it's only my opinion, of course,' said the other, 'but I think it's a hangover from the depression. You see, in those days the firm had to stand off hundreds of men. Obviously, no firm is going to sack their best men if they can help it. Well, the Admiralty step in and take on some of the men stood off so that they won't be lost to the drawing-office side of the shipbuilding industry – and those men are there now. For the most part they're the ones who now have to give official approval of the plans our best men send in!'

But Nicholson and Parnell and their men coped with all the delays and difficulties and brought their ship, for she was theirs and wholly theirs until the Navy actually commissioned her, to a state ready for launching.

On the 5th April, 1939, Lady Henderson, wife of the Admiral who had done so much for the Fleet Air Arm, broke a bottle of champagne wine across the bows of the great ship and said, 'I christen this ship *Illustrious*. May God protect all who sail in her.'

Then, smart and slim in her new grey paint, Britain's latest and greatest aircraft-carrier took to the green water of the Walney Channel. The whole dockyard cheered her, the guests and the men in blue and, above all, those in cap and bowler who had built her, who, a few minutes before, had stood bare-headed to sing 'Eternal Father Strong to Save'.

There she was, floating like a great cygnet, *Illustrious*, No. 732 no longer. For all those who had believed in the Fleet Air Arm and fought with faith and singleness of purpose for that belief, the moment when that long, grey, flat-topped ship floated free on the stream, was a reward – and a promise of further, such moments of consummation to come.

A month after her launch the new Commander of *Illustrious* joined her.

Commander Gerald Seymour Tuck, RN, came of a long and distinguished line of Royal Navy officers going back as far as the seventeenth century. He was a tall, lean, handsome officer, with lively blue eyes and great charm. And there was no mistaking his competence and drive, for Tuck was Royal Navy to his fingertips. He was a gunnery expert who, as a young lieutenant, had headed the field training staff at HMS *Excellent*, the home of naval gunners, and had since had a brilliant career, serving in destroyers and battleships. But he was no stranger to aircraft-carriers either. From November 1930 to September 1931 he had served aboard *Eagle* when she was operating the little Fairey Flycatcher fleet fighters that could do a slow roll straight off the deck. In *Eagle* he had gone to South America for the opening of the British Empire Trade Exhibition on March 14th, 1931, and there had watched the Prince of Wales fly aboard in a Fairey 111F – the first Royal person ever to fly aboard an aircraft-carrier. When he joined *Illustrious* at Barrow he brought something of the *Eagle* and the old Fleet Air Arm with him, something of the spirit of his old Commander-in-Chief's farewell speech to *Eagle*'s ship's company, when he said:

'I want you to think of the commission you have just done not as being over, but rather remaining, for what you have done in this ship will have a lasting effect in the Service....Take with you what you have learned in the *Eagle*; that is the way the Service goes on. What has been done does not disappear; it remains in the minds of those you leave behind and you must carry it on to your new ships.

Illustrious was a very new ship, the first of a new line. When Tuck received his appointment to her he was serving in HMS *Nelson* as Fleet Gunnery Officer on the staff of Admiral Sir Roger Backhouse. He took up the appointment in May.

The 'Commander' is the executive officer of a big warship. He runs the ship and is responsible to the Captain for her efficiency and well-being in every department. It is the Captain's duty to use the ship as a weapon to fight with, the Commander's to make sure that he has an efficient weapon to use. When Tuck arrived at Barrow he found that the ship's main machinery and eight 4.5-inch twin turrets had been installed, but that the whole fitting out of *Illustrious*' internal compartments, living, spaces for officers and men, storerooms, bridge fittings, aircraft launching and arrester gear and many other vital details, were still outstanding. He took his coat off, rolled up his sleeves and pitched in with Parnell, Nicholson and all the others.

The firm's men were still hard at it. With the ship afloat in the Walney Channel, tugs seized her and towed her along to the fitting-out basin in Buccleugh Dock, where they would need the giant one-hundred-and-fifty-ton crane to lift the boilers and main engines into the ship. The loose sections of the flight deck were unbolted, and a great plant of 110,000 horsepower lowered piece by piece into the empty shell. With her engines installed, the deck above was, closed again, plates finally riveted and fixed and work immediately begun to raise the slim tower of the bridge island on the starboard side of the flight deck.

To build this, Parnell laid down railway tracks along the flight deck to carry a seven-ton travelling steam crane. But he had to shore up the deck first, putting great baulks of timber underneath the deep beams that bore the armour plating up. 'Get away!' they said. 'When you build a flight deck it ought to be able to stand *any* weight without crutches!'

So the island rose, the brain of the ship, and her final shape filled out and fitted into the Barrow landscape like some new addition to her civic buildings.

She lay with her great, flaring, square-topped bows almost abutting the wide swing-bridge that joined Barrow Island and the works with the mainland. People stopped on the bridge to gape at her, the biggest, most powerful ship they had ever seen, and the strangest. Among these was a young man named Norman Hanson, who used to come over to Barrow from Whitehaven every Saturday afternoon to meet his pal Ray and go to the rugger match, for Barrow turns out greet rugger players as well as fine ships. When he got there nowadays he nearly always found time to go and see how they were getting on with the new aircraft-carrier. The ship attracted him as part of the fascination which the sea had always had for him, and the thought that they could fly aeroplanes from this strange vessel intrigued him. What is more, he had the sort of twinkle in his eye and the dash and verve which in England so readily makes civil servants like himself into good sailors.

And it was midsummer, 1939. Norman read his paper and listened to the wireless like everybody else.

On August 24th came Mr Chamberlain's statement to the nation that 'We find ourselves confronted with the imminent peril of war.' A Nazi gauleiter had been thrust upon the 'free' city of Danzig and proclaimed as head of the State – a climax in the rising surge of German and Italian power that had already engulfed Czechoslovakia, part of Lithuania, and Albania. And now Hitler's eyes were fixed on Poland. By grabbing Danzig, the sea outlet for Polish overseas trade, he hoped to throttle the country. At the same time he increased his flood of hysterical vituperation of Britain and France for their rearmament and their opposition to his desires for more and more *Lebensraum* at the expense of the peaceful countries of Europe. The situation became so volatile that on March 31st Britain and France signed an agreement to support Poland if Germany attacked her, and a month later a Conscription Bill was passed in the House of Commons.

If it meant conscription for him and his age group, thought Norman Hanson, then he would go into the Navy, if the office would release him. He had a hankering to go on one of those new aircraft-carriers....

The news in the papers grew graver, the headlines bigger and blacker. In mid-August the German puppet government of Danzig began to stop, Polish customs officials from carrying out their duties. Poland protested, only to receive more German threats. Then the Nazis assumed control of the Danzig Senate and increased their threats even further. The Pope, President Roosevelt and the King of the Belgians all made broadcast appeals for peace. But it seemed that nothing could avert war now.

The Royal Navy was mobilised, the Reserve Fleet recalled for extensive combined sea and, air 'exercises', and the ships of the Home Fleet put to sea ready for any eventuality.

In all the shipyards of Britain the tempo of work was increased. Many of the ships that would be vitally needed if war did break out were only half-finished, many others were still only dreams on a draughtsman's board.

Aboard the new carrier in Buccleugh Dock at Barrow, work went steadily on. Commander Tuck worked himself and everybody else hard to finish the ship. One by one other officers began to arrive, men like Bill Acworth, the Gunnery Officer, Ralph Duckworth, the Torpedo Officer; Commander (E) Tamplin, the Chief Engineering Officer; Mr Guttridge, the commissioned Shipwright; and 'Rosy' Baker, the new First Lieutenant. Whenever some new fitting was to be put into the ship the firm's man in charge would ask Tuck just how and where he wanted it installed. Tuck would consult his technical officer concerned and, with the approval of the Principal Ship Overseer, who was the link between the Admiralty and the ship's technical officers, the thing was done forthwith. This was a realistic interpretation of the official set-up, according to which the ship's future officers were only there to 'watch' the firm putting the techinical equipment in and to witness firm's trial of it.

It had always been the intention that *Illustrious* should be completed with all the peacetime embellishments that a first-class shipbuilding yard like Vickers-Armstrongs was prepared to put into her, and Sir Charles Craven and the yard held good to this intention throughout her completion. Soon after Tuck bad come up to Barrow, Sir Charles took him aside and said to him:

'Look here, I'll give you additional items such as special wood panelling and gratings and so on for the officers' and mens' quarters. They won't be shown on the bill from my firm.'

This attitude on the part of the firm helped enormously to make the new carrier something special in the line of smart, tiddley ships. The fact that she was an aircraft-carrier was not going to be allowed to make her a mere floating garage for aeroplanes. She was going to be the last word, Hitler or no Hitler.

Her Commander had in many ways to be a sort of combination of housekeeper and housemaster. Besides supervising the running of the whole ship from these her earliest beginnings, he was responsible for furnishing and equipping her as well. The Admiralty was quite reasonably indulgent in the matter of furnishings, and costing limits allowed for very good materials to be chosen. When it came to the point, Mrs Tuck did most of the choosing of this sort of thing for her husband's new ship, and the men of the *Illustrious* benefited much from her taste. Between them, she and the Commander would decide on this or that carpeting, linoleum or curtain material, this kind of wood or that, and the firm would order the goods, for *Illustrious* was the yard's ship yet.

Everybody spent much time, much loving care and attention over the detailed plans of the various layouts in the ship. Great care was taken, for example, in the design of the ship's chapel, a quiet corner of the ship which was to play an important part in her life. For better organisation each department in the ship was allotted its own special colour, and for ease of identification all plans were coloured according to departments, as were all the secondary lights in the compartments themselves, the same colour scheme being used to great advantage later on in the damage control organisation.

The bridge island was up now, and with it the funnel, the masts, the various conning platforms and all the offices of the air department located there. Everywhere the pieces were going in faster and faster as the tempo of completion increased. The puzzle was nearing its solution when...

'From Admiralty to all concerned at home and abroad. Most immediate. Commence hostilities at once with Germany.'

And then it was '*Hurry, hurry, hurry*, get her finished and away before the Germans come and bomb her. Never mind the trimmings now – *Illustrious* is at war.'

CHAPTER TWO

A Famous Victory

'...The ships we need to win the war with must be in commission in 1940.

'Pray throw yourselves into this and give me your aid to smooth away the obstacles.'

Thus the First Lord of the Admiralty, Mr Winston Churchill, – to the First Sea Lord and others on October 8th, 1939. 'The above remarks,' he said, 'apply also to the aircraft carriers.'

The war was a month old. Already our carriers had been in action. At this stage they were being used singly as the nucleus of U-boat hunting killer groups, whose main use was to protect the many merchant ships caught at sea on the outbreak of war which were now making for our ports. Ten days after the declaration of war *Ark Royal*, with three destroyers, sank U-39 one hundred and fifty miles west of the Hebrides.

Three days after this, however, fortune swung the other way. The new flotilla leader *Kelly*, Captain Lord Louis Mountbatten, chasing a submarine contact in heavy weather off Land's End, picked up an SOS from the *Courageous*, which had been patrolling the South Western Approaches. She and four destroyers had been steaming in the approaches to the Bristol Channel on the evening of the 17th when she picked up a signal from a merchant ship which was being attacked by a U-boat. She at once detached two of her escorts to chase the U-boat. At dusk she turned into wind to fly on a patrol of her Swordfish, and in doing so presented a shadowing U-boat with the best target her captain could have wished for. Two torpedoes hit the unprotected side of the carrier and she began to go down. All ships in the vicinity raced to her aid and managed to pull over seven hundred of her men out of the icy sea and choking scum of oil fuel and petrol. Over five hundred men were lost with the veteran carrier.

There was more urgent need than ever now for the new carriers, especially the one so near. completion at Barrow.

More of *Illustrious*' officers had now arrived. Her new First Lieutenant, with his experience as First Lieutenant of the battleship *Queen Elizabeth*, was already proving the brilliant organising ability. Most important of all, the foundations of her air department had now been soundly laid.

'Streamline' Robertson learned to fly an aeroplane in 1924.

He went to Netheravon with the first naval officers to volunteer for the new Fleet Air Arm, and qualified as a naval pilot by landing an old Avro Bison aboard the narrow deck of the *Argus* a year later. Afterwards he went to the *Furious*, and later to the *Eagle*. In 1934 he was in *Courageous*, and the following year in *Glorious*, and it was aboard her, then under Captain Rawlings, and later under Captain Bruce Prater, that the serious practice of torpedo attacks against warships really began. Robertson's career had thus far been closely representative of the development of the Fleet Air Arm itself, and in June 1939 he joined *Illustrious*, to be her first Commander (Air).

He had already had a month in *Ark Royal* during the spring cruise, and had noted in particular her new 'crash barrier', a system of cables stretched across the deck abreast the bridge island, which could be raised to stop aircraft on the deck which had missed the arrester wires. The use of the barrier meant that an aircraft could land behind it at the same time as the one which had previously landed was being struck down into the hangar in front of it via the forward lift. The whole process was thus enormously speeded up. At the same time a technique of deck-landing control was coming into favour with the Royal Navy, in which an officer stood at the after end of the night deck and guided an approaching aircraft on to the deck by a system of signals with two 'bats' held in his outstretched hands. This process, which was by no means new, had been forced into general favour by the prospect of faster, more modern aircraft.

The Fifth Sea Lord had gloomily forecast forty per cent casualties as a result of using the barrier technique and Robertson had been so incautious as to say 'Nonsense!' to the great man's face. He knew that what the Americans could do we could do. All it needed was a little discipline.

During his month with *Ark Royal* he formed the firm resolution that things would be different in *Illustrious*.

'You know what that is down there?' asked Captain Power, pointing to *Ark*'s single barrier. 'You won't have one of those things.'

'Oh yes we shall, sir,' said Streamline, 'we shall have two.'

'Then I bet you'll never use 'em,' said Power.

'By God we will!' said Robertson under his breath, 'if I have anything to do with it, and we'll have a batsman too!'

Ark Royal still did things the old-fashioned way, without using barrier or batsman, and consequently her squadrons took a long time to land on. It wouldn't be done that way in *Illustrious*, vowed Streamline. He remembered *Courageous* in the days when Alex Ramsay was Rear-Admiral, Aircraft Carriers. Ramsay was a far-seeing man who had foreseen the danger in battle of a slow land-on and had ordered his squadrons to be batted aboard. Robertson himself had used the bats before at Gosport and was confident that he could land aircraft with them, as he said, 'on a half-crown!'

He left *Ark Royal* in March and went up to Newcastle-upon-Tyne to join the staff of the Admiral Superintendent, Contract-Built Ships, there, to help him with the supervision of the new carriers building, before joining *Illustrious* himself at Barrow. He visited the carriers building on the Tyne, at Barrow and at Belfast, then went to Barrow to join his ship in June, a month after Tuck, her Executive Commander, had joined her. Streamline was determined that he would do his utmost to see that this ship really was run as an *aircraft*-carrier, not like a battleship with the accent on guns. The organisation of a carrier's air department he knew from *Glorious* and *Ark Royal*. Now, however, he had to set to and build his own. Like the other department heads, he turned to 'watch' the fitting out and to gain the confidence of the builders so as to get his own department off to a good start. He was alone in the air department until October, when Douglas Russell, his assistant, and the future batsman of the ship, arrived and soon proved a tower of strength. Then the new Air Staff Officer, George Beale, came and in February 1940 Lieutenant Gregory, the armament expert.

The First Lieutenant had worked wonders in a short time organising messdecks in preparation for the big draft of ratings which would be joining the ship in the near future. As the advance parties of technical ratings and seamen arrived, it soon became clear that a tremendous spirit of enthusiasm and eagerness to commission and get to sea as soon as possible quickened every effort.

So it happened that when her first Captain joined her he found a keen, hard-working team already in possession. Such was the new Captain's personality that his arrival added greater impetus to the hustling spirit aboard.

Captain Denis Boyd left his home in the south of England for *Illustrious* in February 1940, at the beginning of the bad snowfall of that year. The snow halted him halfway to the ship and kept him and his wife stranded in a seedy hold for some days. Eventually, however, they reached Carnforth Junction and changed trains for Barrow. Just as the train was about to pull out, Boyd saw a chief petty officer struggling with bag and hammock on the icy platform; he immediately leapt down on to the platform, flung bag and hammock into his own compartment and bundled the flabbergasted chid in after them. The latter was even more astonished when he found himself in the same compartment as his new Captain, and Captain Boyd was somewhat surprised himself to find that he had landed his own Chief Gunner's Mate. He was a worthwhile catch, and the incident was a good start to the commission.

Boyd was a thwarted naval aviator. Early in 1911 the Aero Club of Great Britain generously offered to teach four naval officers to fly. The offer was accepted by the Admiralty and Lieutenant-Commander Samson, Lieutenant Gregory, Lieutenant Longmore and Lieutenant Gerrard of the Royal Marines, became the first British naval aviators. The new Air Department of the Navy, begun by Murray Sueter, the youngest Captain in the Navy List, had a number of enthusiastic volunteers. One of them was Denis Boyd. He applied to join naval aviation in 1911 and at Eastchurch, Samson allowed him to fly a Bristol Pusher aircraft. But the new branch only took three new entries a year and Boyd was only one of nineteen applicants. In fact he had a serious battle with his Captain, who did everything he could to prevent a very promising young officer from indulging in what he looked upon as a ridiculous adventure. No more volunteers had been absorbed into the Air Department by the time war broke out in 1914, so Boyd tried destroyers. He had actually been appointed in command of an 'oily wad' torpedo boat when he was sent instead, much against his will, to do a long torpedo course at HMS *Vernon*. After *Vernon* he asked for submarines and spent the rest of the war with Captain Little in the steam-propelled 'K' boats. About 1930 he began to realise how far short of naval requirements the RAF-dominated Fleet Air Arm really was. He knew many people in naval aviation and began to bend his own efforts towards improving it. When he was appointed in 1934 as Director of the Tactical Division, he gathered together what he considered to be the best men in the Admiralty at the time and they made out, as a committee, a report on the future of naval aviation. Boyd also had a hand in preparing the paper which really succeeded in getting the Fleet Ait Arm back into naval hands, and it tell to him to lobby it a great deal. As DTD he was also very much concerned with the staff requirements of the new *Illustrious* and her immediate successors, and it was a logical and fitting thing when he was appointed to *Illustrious* herself in command.

When he first set eyes upon his ship she lay listed over with the great weight of snow on her flight deck. Aboard, everything seemed at first rusty and unready. Her Captain walked her sloping decks and thought of other ships he had joined, of the beautiful *Hood* and the trim, rakish *Hardy*, the fine destroyer which he had commanded in the Mediterranean. He thought, *When a ship is fitting out you reach the ultimate of despair and frustration. You cannot believe that any order or decency can ever be created in her. She is a hulk then, like this one. But it doesn't last, the hulk always comes to life. And this ship is rustling with life already, groping out for greatness. May I help to bring this greatness to her.*

The very impact of her name suggested glory, and her crest, inherited from the old *L'Illustre*, captured from the French in tha tune of Nelson, was three brazen trumpets. The Captain pondered this, then asked his brother, a classical scholar, 'to think of a motto involving God and War', because, as he said, 'If I don't have a motto linking those trumpets with God and War they'll be connected with blowing hard!'

His brother looked in the Scriptures and found a sentence of St Paul which ran:

'And if the trumpet hath an uncertain sound who shall arm himself for the battle?'

From this they took the Latin *'Vox Non Incerta'*, 'No Un-certain Sound', and made it the motto of *Illustrious*. Her men took great heart from this inspired choice and me new team worked on with greater zest than ever.

Once he had met his officers and the firm's representatives and inspected the ship there was not a great deal for the Captain to do. What was left outstanding was Tuck's job. Boyd's job was not to run the ship, but to fight it, and his weapons were his air squadrons. These had now been formed and were working up at air stations all over Britain, so the Captain went on a tour to watch their progress and let them all know what he expected of them.

There were three squadrons waiting to join *Illustrious*, Nos. 815 and 819 Swordfish Torpedo Bomber Squadrons, commanded by Lieutenant-Commander R A Kilroy, DSC, and Lieutenant-Commander J W Hale, and No. 806 Fighter Squadron under Lieutenant-Commander C L G Evans, DSC.

These men were all officers of great dash, skill and accomplishment

Evans had led the flight of Skuas from *Ark Royal*, which had shot down a Dornier three weeks after the outbreak of war – the first enemy aircraft destroyed. He had left 803 Squadron in *Ark Royal* to form 806 for the new *Illustrious* at Worthy Down, in Hampshire. From here they flew their Skuas to West Freugh, in Scotland, for intensive working up.

'Ginger' Hale had formed 819 at Ford, in Sussex, then they too had gone up to West Freugh for air gunnery practice. After three weeks here they went back to Ford, Any *ex-Glorious* man who came in contact with 819 might have made an inspired guess as to what the Admiralty had in mind for *Illustrious*. For he would have recognised many faces – 'John Willy' Hale himself, 'Blood' Scarlet and 'Tiffy' Torrens-Spence, that very thrusting pilot, Clifford and 'Grubby' Going, Hamilton, Sutton, Lea and Skelton. All these men had been in *Glorious* under Lumley Lyster, and they all knew what to do to the Italian Fleet. They were the backbone of the squadron, experienced RN pilots and observers who would be a great source of strength to the new RNVR's, of which Hale had four pilots and four observers.

Robin Kilroy, CO of 815, was *ex-Glorious*, too. He and Hale were both specialists in leading mose Lumley Lyster specials – night torpedo attacks. Others, like Dick Janvrin, one of 815's observers, had come from *Ark Royal*. In fact mere was not one carrier in the Fleet unrepresented.

Captain Boyd not only watched the squadrons' work, he took part in it, flying with them as often as he could and reflecting, after an extremely athletic hour in the back seat of 'Ginger' Hale's Swordfish, that dive-bombing was not the most restful of occupations. He also found time, before he returned to his ship for good to go aboard *Ark Royal* and watch her operating aircraft. There he was seriously advised not to use 'the crash barrier' aboard *Illustrious*. It was too dangerous, they told him. That didn't seem to square up with what his Commander (Air) had told him, but he would take that up with the forceful Streamline when he rejoined the ship.

Back aboard *Illustrious* the 'Chicago pianos' – the new pom-poms – were put in and manned by a few key ratings throughout the night, while German bombers droned overhead in the inky blackness, circling.... The guns aboard followed their movements round but kept silent for fear of drawing down bombs upon their new ship. The Gunner himself worried as well about a small furnished house on Walney Island where he had recently installed Mrs Banham.

The completion date for the ship was postponed for a month so that the crash barriers would be installed. Streamline Robertson rubbed his hands. The opportunity was also taken to put up a stump mast at the after end of the bridge island to carry the new Radio Direction Finding aerials. This early radar would make the new carrier an especially priceless addition to the Fleet. In the same month the aircraft catapult was put in and Streamline saw the last piece in his own special puzzle fall into place. He fairly jittered to put all his new gadgets into, action – batsman, barrier and catapult all working together, landing, striking down and launching planes in one swift, well-oiled action, like the parts of a stopwatch with his thumb on the plunger.

Other last-minute additions and alterations were made and acceptance officers arrived from the various technical departments of the Admiralty to look over the nearly completed work of art which was *Illustrious*. More key ratings arrived and a warmly welcomed handful of RAF aircraft maintenance men to make up for the technical ratings which the new Fleet Air Arm had had no time to train. Bill Banham had half a dozen of these attached to fais hardworking Gunner's Party. Then the main body of tfae ship's company arrived and filled the mess-decks with noise and clatter. There was a general settling in and sorting out. For the first time life began to stir and throb throughout the whole great ship.

Dock trials had begun as long ago as January. On the 29th steam was raised for the first time on one boiler. Then, item by item, me list was checked off – bomb lifts and watertight doors, fresh cold water systems and main protected bulkhead, auxiliary machinery in the boiler rooms, turbo-generators, pumping systems and the fire-proof curtains, made like Venetian shutters in steel, which divided, the hangar into three sub-hangars, air compressors and cool drinking water systems, steam-heating arrangements, messing and sleeping quarters, washplaces, sanitary arrangements and sick bay. There were preliminary capstan and anchor trials, tests of the electrical communications, of ammunition conveyors and aircraft lifts, of arrester gear and hangar-spraying arrangements, of hydrophones and wireless equipment, of galley and bakery fittings, even of pantry bells and dish-washing machines.

Then, on Tuesday, April 16th, the main body of personnel arrived and slept and were victualled aboard for the first time.

And on that day *Illustrious* commissioned. Her Captain signed for her, the White Ensign was hoisted for the first time, and she became a unit of the Royal Navy.

On Monday 22nd she left her berth for Ramsden Dock, and next day moved into her deep-water berth. On the 24th she put out to pick up her escort at Lightning Knoll Buoy and head for Liverpool.

On the way she swung compasses, calibrated her pitometer log, tested her echo sounder and once out in open water, tried out her steering gear, from hard over to hard over. She was wasting no time.

At Liverpool she went into the Gladstone Dock to have her underwater fittings finally cheeked, her bilge keels fitted and the cast-iron temporary propellers which had brought her from Barrow exchanged for the real thing. Her paravane equipment was tested, her bottom and boot-tapping painted and there were tests, trials and inspections of a great assortment of fittings, among them the radar, fire-control circuits, crash barriers, cinema arrangements, the typhoon whistle and the sirens, the engine and boiler-room electrical communications, telegraphs, steering gear, aircraft signalling and gunnery equipment. Even awnings and canvas covers were inspected, though no one expected, to use them.

Captain Boyd sent for Bill Banham. How long would it take to fuse his outfit of ammunition, expected on board at any time?

'Fourteen days, sir,' sail Bill immediately, 'working from six in the morning until six at night.'

The Captain was surprised but he knew his Gunner well enough by now not to question his judgement. And Bill had in fact worked out the time down to a question of minutes per round, having done the whole process himself on a dummy round. Then it arrived, high explosive and semi-armour piercing, smoke, star-shell and pom-pom. Bill's area for fusing all this was limited by the extent of the flight deck, and each fusing party had to be just so many yards apart, 'just in case.' The key men of the Gunner's Party beat all records to finish this delicate and dangerous job. Shortly afterwards the guns were fired at sea for the first time.

All was done at tfae rush, for the situation was urgent. Hitler had invaded Denmark and Norway. The 'phoney war' was over. In Norway the RAF was unable to operate until airfields could be established, and the carriers and planes of the Fleet Air Arm once more came into their own. *Courageous* had been sunk by a U-boat in the second week of war, but *Furious*, *Glorious* and *Ark Royal* were hurriedly sent to Norwegian waters where, their bombers and fighters gave desperately needed support to our 'Norwegian Expeditionary Force'.

It was thus desperately urgent that the new carrier should get to sea. In fact, as the situation in Norway grew hourly more tense, *Illustrious* narrowly escaped being sent there, incomplete and unprepared as she was, to do what she could. Her contribution could have been but little. She had no aircraft, and no means of operating any. To send a fine new carrier against the full fury of four hundred German bombers was a ridiculous and suicidal risk, and Captain Boyd risked his career by refusing point-blank to take her out on such a foolhardy mission.

It was a good thing that the Admiralty listened to him. Otherwise

Illustrious might have gone the way of the *Glorious*. For now that brave, happy and historic ship had been lost. On the 3rd of June she and *Ark Royal* had arrived off Narvik, the *Ark* to provide fighter protection and security patrols; over tfae troops and transports of the evacuation force, *Glorious* to re-embark some of the R.A.F. fighters she had brought to Norway only a few days before. By a strange and appropriate coincidence Lumley Lyster was directly involved in this last operation of his old ship. In fact he was the only one who believed that this operation could be done. The eighteen Hurricanes had been given up as lost until Lyster, ashore in Norway, insisted that they could be flown aboard *Glorious*, unhooked as they were and with their pilots completely untrained in carrier landings. He was right. One machine hit the funnel and one went over the side, but sixteen landed on safely. Then, a few hours later, he learned to his great sorrow that his beloved *Glorious* had been sunk by the *Scharnhorst* and *Gneisenau* before she could fly off her aircraft. All but twenty-five of the men aboard her were lost.

After more checks and inspections. *Illustrious* left dry dock and went out for sea trials. These were cut as short as efficiency permitted. In fact her orders bore the footnote, 'If an extra day's trial can be so avoided the Cruising Trial and Full Power Trial may be of four hours' duration each.'

Passing the Bar Light Vessel at one o'clock they began their stepped-up programme – preuminary full-power trial, steering-gear trials at full power and cruising power, and the cruising trial at twenty-three knots, together with armament trials. Then followed arrester-gear trials and finally a full-power trial, with the ship working up to her fast maximum speed of thirty knots. At the end ot trials, without more ado she steamed for Spithead, where she anchored on the morning of May 26th, 1940.

Now the Germans were all around us. Norway had fallen to them, with all its long seaboard facing me east coasts of Britain, Holland and Belgium were beaten nations and France was breaking. There was only one bright-sign in the sky. Winston Churchill was at No. 10. And there was still the Navy.

It was obviously only a matter of days before Mussolini cashed in on his partner's enterprise. The Battle Fleet moved back from home waters into the Mediterranean, to be joined there by cruisers from the East Indies, some submarines from China and the aircraft-carrier *Eagle*.

This carrier was now alone in the 'Italian lake', the sole representative of the Fleet Air Arm afloat there, with the whole weight of the *Regia Aeronautica* about to fall upon our few planes and ships – an old ship with a handful of aircraft to defend the Fleet, including four old Sea Gladiators, originally meant for the *Glorious*. These four were the only fighters in the Fleet.

And now *Illustrious'* fighters and bombers were in the battle. Evans, after bringing the fighter squadron to the peak of efficiency had suffered the intense chagrin of watching his best pilots being taken from him and whirled into the desperate fighting in Norway. In vain he protested to the Admiralty against this ruthless breaking up of a first-class squadron. He was told to make the best of it, and promised that whatever happened 806 would be preserved for *Illustrious*. He received as replacements some of the very first RNVR pilots to join the Navy. At least they were keen, if far less experienced than his old RN pilots. The squadron was moved to Hatston in the Orkneys, and from there they went over in their Skuas to bomb Bergen. It was a long and dangerous haul and there was never more than twenty minutes' fuel left in their tanks on their return, no matter how clever a pilot was with his engine control. Some engines even cut out on landing, their tanks drained of the very last spoonful of petrol.

From Norway they were switched, with no pause for rest, to attack targets across the Channel as Hitler invaded the Low Countries. There was a grave shortage of aircraft now, and by the end of May seven naval squadrons had been lent to Coastal Command. Evans' Skuas flew from Detling alongside Hale's Swordfish, and operated their obsolete machines as fighters on a standing patrol line along the French coast to Dunkirk. There were never more than four of them on patrol at a time, and the four Skuas had to share their beat with eighteen Messerschmitt 109's. Hale's squadron did anti-submarine patrols and laid mines in enemy waters. They all began to wonder whether they would ever see *Illustrious*.

However, early in June they did see her, lying below on a shimmering sea off Plymouth. As they circled the ship awaiting the signal to land on, they could see plainly the new crash barrier, the first time most of them had ever seen one and the first time any of them had faced the prospect of working with this reputedly dangerous gadget.

Streamline Robertson was adamant that it should be used, but the Captain was not sure.

'Look here,' he said, 'it's all very well for you to tell me the thing's all right. The people in *Ark Royal* say it isn't. Who am I to believe?'

'You believe me, sir,' said Streamline. 'I know it will work.'

'Well, do you mind not using it the first time,' said Boyd.

But Robertson, Douglas Russell, who would be batting the new boys on, Peter Gregory and Commander Colin Mitchell from McTaggart, Scott's, who had fitted the flight-deck gear in, went into a huddle over a glass of gin. Next morning Streamline went to the Captain with the light of battle in his eye and said, as firmly as he knew bow:

'I've thought about the barrier, sir, and I'd like,to use it.'

The Swordfish, with their slow and steady ways, got aboard without any trouble. Charles Evans came on in the first Skua and hooted on with his usual skill. The second one made a bad landing, however, missed the arrester wires and was pulled up short by the barrier. The barrier stopped several more that day, too, although no one was hurt. The fighters were a mixed bag of Skuas and Fulmars, the new three-hundred-knot Fleet fighters. These were being flown in many cases by green young RNVR pilots who had scarcely even seen the new machines before. As one of them said to Bill Banham, 'We were told to hop in and get aboard.' Half a dozen of the brand-new machines were smashed up in these early landings through inexperience, with spares and replacements non-existent, and each machine worth £8,000, according to the Fairey Aviation representative, on board – more than the price of a Spitfire at a time when urgent appeals were being made for Spitfire funds to fight the impending Battle of Britain. The crashing aircraft also smashed a 4.5-inch director tower and most of its instruments and put one of the pom-pom mountings out of action. There were no spares for these either.

There was still one stage to go through before *Illustrious* joined a war zone. After final storing and preparation she put out of Plymouth Sound and headed, with destroyer escort, for the open Atlantic and Bermuda to carry out final working-up trials.

Darkened and zig-zagging she entered the Bay of Biscay in the teeth of a heavy head sea. Seas crashed against the broad flare of her bows and suddenly, in the first watch, near midnight, a foc's'le messdeck scuttle smashed in and the green sea poured in. Mr Guttridge rushed with his team of shipwrights to the spot to shore up the split scuttle. Then another one gave, and another, until six or seven were shattered. The fort messdecks, pride of 'Rosy' Baker's delight, were awash. All night the shipwright's squads wrestled with the terrible job of plugging and shoring the scuttles, cursing and blinding the new light alloy they had been made from. Outside, the sea howled and raged, tearing and beating at the new ship.

In the western Atlantic the weather worsened. Gear was smashed all over the ship and a thirty-two-foot cutter washed overboard. More scuttles were store in, the searchlight platforms for'd were punched into a permanent upward tilt by breaking seas, and the anti-magnetic-mine degaussing belt was ripped into a forlorn tatter of flapping Irish pennants round the ship's side. The destroyer escort was ordered home and the ship thrust on alone to Bermuda.

She was the biggest ship this lovely island had ever seen, and Captain

Boyd had to handle her very carefully, easing her on main engines alone through the narrow entrance to the inner harbour, for fear her rudder would swing her on to the rocks.

That evening, to everyone's amazement. Lord Haw-Haw announced;

'HMS *Illustrious* has been torpedoed by a German U-boat.'

The date of the 'attack' was given, July 4th, even the name of the U-boat commander. First Lieutenant Endras. When, later, the *BBC* denied the sinking of the *Illustrious*, Haw-Haw promptly replied;

'It was not claimed that she was sunk, but that she was hit by torpedo,' and went on to say, 'HMS *Illustrious* is at present carrying out repairs in Bermuda Bay.'

He was right, but the repairs had been caused by heavy weather, not by Lieutenant Endras' torpedo. However, it was disconcerting to realise that the Germans knew exactly where the ship was.

These scares and wild rumours worried wives and mothers at home much more than the men themselves. On one occasion the Captain's wife was walking down a London street, making her way to Victoria to catch her train home, when she suddenly saw a blackboard propped up against a news-stand bearing the words:

'*Illustrious* sunk with all hands.'

Seriously alarmed she walked on, caught her train and, by the time she had reached home, felt just about up to dealing with the telephone. Besides her own anxiety, she was worried about the effect of the news upon the wives and mothers of her husband's men. However, when the Admiralty told her they knew nothing, she felt immensely relieved. The 'news' was obviously a mere scare, but she felt angry at the irresponsible sensationalism that had probably caused anxiety and suffering.

At Bermuda the Swordfish flew every day but one. With their slow speed and gear lift they could easily be operated with the ship stationary in harbour. All that was wanted was a tug to heave the ship round into wind. But the fighters could not get off unless there was a really good breeze. After an early scare in Plymouth when a machine took off with only eight knots of wind and all but hit the sea, it was laid down by Robertson that there must be at least thirteen knots of wind before they could operate.

One Sunday morning in Bermuda someone said, 'Seventeen knots. What about the fighters?'

'Yes, good show,' said Streamline. 'Go ahead. Buck up their morale!'

Off went six Skuas and two Fulmars. But the wind died before they could land on again. Both types of machine had a speed of entry of sixty knots. With no wind to brake them down they would almost certainly rip their hooks out and crash all over the deck.

Everybody, waited, praying for a capful of wind, With the fighters circling overhead, rapidly running out of fuel.

Eventually, with petrol almost gone, they were nagged in. Still no wind.

The two Fulmars and two of the Skuas got on safely, but the other four were not so lucky and all pulled their hooks out. One came in and piled up abreast the island. One finished up right in the eyes of the ship with its tail hanging over the port side, and a third went right over the bows into the sea. They called that day Black Sunday. It was a miracle that no one was hurt.

The last pilot of the four, Roger Nicholls, came in, felt his hook part company with the fuselage, opened up and climbed away.   .

Hasty signals passed between him and the ship. The best place for him to land seemed to be the soft green acres of the nearby Mid Ocean Golf Club.

'Hole out on the seventeenth green!' signalled Captain Boyd.

Nicholls took him literally. In landing, his wing hit a tree, the plane broke up and its engine finished neatly on the smooth turf of the seventeenth green.

This could have been embarrassing, but Charles Evans reversed the situation adroitly by presenting the battered engine to the Club as a souvenir. He did this with such charm that the members were convinced that a great honour was being bestowed upon them. The rest of the pieces he collected and had brought back to the ship in the only lorry available on Bermuda.

They spent a few days and nights at sea training all those who had no experience of night-flying tactics. The old hands showed the way, with Streamline Robertson, who had once served with Hale's old squadron in the *Glorious*, driving them on.

Then, with a new degaussing strip in position and good solid brass scuttles fitted in place of the flimsy alloy ones. *Illustrious* sailed for home. There was plenty of flying on the way, mainly to get the fighter boys happy about landing on behind the carrier.

By the time she got home she was a thoroughly well worked up ship and even Streamline and the Captain seemed fairly satisfied.

As soon as the ship reached England, Boyd found himself summoned to the Admiralty. As soon as he arrived he realised that he was in for some disturbing news because his old friend Dudley Pound, now First Sea Lord, immediately shook him by the hand, a thing he had never done in twenty-four years of friendship. What was said confirmed his foreboding.

'I want you,' said Pound, 'in view of the desperate situation to take

Illustrious through the Strait's of Gibraltar and join Andrew. He needs you badly out there.'

Boyd caught a whiff of fear as he heard the words, for he knew exactly what they implied. Mussolini, with his air fleet and powerful navy, was massing his troops in Africa for the big offensive against Egypt and General Wavell's army. But the Captain knew what a tremendous help his Swordfish and the fresh consignment of Fulmars they were putting aboard would be to Admiral Cunningham, and how priceless the new radar he carried would be in giving warning to enemy spotting aircraft and bombers. In such a situation *Illustrious* would draw Italian bombs as an apple attracts maggots. They would need that armoured flight deck.

The urgent need for more air cover in the Mediterranean had started when Italy came into the war in June, for the Italian Fleet heavily outnumbered our own and was far more modern.

At the end of July the situation had deteriorated further. The enemy began to increase his reconnaissance nights over the Fleet anchorage at Alexandria. When the British Fleet was reported in harbour the Italians would send more fast convoys of reinforcements across to Libya.

The Commander-in-Chief did what he could to stop enemy preparations. Our few submarines attacked Italian convoys in the dangerously clear and shallow waters between Italy and North Africa; the Battle Fleet bombarded encampments, barracks and batteries at Bardia and the gunboat *Ladybird* shelled the port at point-blank range; in a surprise night attack our destroyers shot up the seaplane base at Bomba, and three Fleet Air Arm Swordfish sank two submarines, a destroyer and a depot ship in Bomba Bay.

But these attacks were not enough. To reduce the odds it was decided to send the new *Illustrious*, the battleship *Valiant* and the anti-aircraft cruisers *Calcutta* and *Coventry* to the Mediterranean.

The *Eagle*, which had joined the Fleet in May, was not up to the task of defending the whole Fleet. Her comparatively limited fuel endurance was adequate for the narrow waters of the Mediterranean, but she was twenty years old and her speed and armour were far below modern requirements. Neither did she have the up-to-date fittings of the later carriers. She was not equipped to operate fighters, and when she acquired four Sea Gladiator fighters from Malta she was hard put to use them.

There were no fighter pilots to fly the machines, but Commander Keighley-Peach, Commander (Flying), of the *Eagle*, trained two Swordfish pilots and these three men went up to protect the Fleet.

For a while the Commander flew alone, one man against an Air Force, the only fighter over the Fleet. Once he took off with bullet in his thigh and shot down an enemy aircraft. In all they destroyed eleven enemy machines between them.

For three months the *Eagle* was alone. Her brood went up again and again, from her scarred wooden decks and from rough airstrips in the desert, hitting the enemy hard.

Then *Illustrious* came.

She sailed, in company with *Valiant*, from Scapa Flow at the end of August. Mrs Boyd missed seeing her husband before he left. They had hoped to be able to celebrate their silver wedding anniversary together, but *Illustrious* went in such a hurry that they never saw each other. Aboard the carrier, going out as Rear-Admiral, Aircraft-Carriers, Mediterranean, was, significantly, Lumley Lysler himself. It was easy to guess what was in the wind, especially for all the old Glorious pilots.

815 Squadron had a new CO Robin Kilroy had been promoted and had left the ship, to be replaced by Lieutenant-Commander Kenneth Williamson, a very experienced naval pilot, who had been in the old *Courageous*, now at the bottom of the Atlantic, in the days of the first arrester-wire trials. He well remembered making many a dart at the deck wondering which of three different experimental wires would catch his hook – a race which was won in the end by the hydraulic type which now, in an improved form, spanned *Illustrious* flight deck.

The pilots were recalled at the rush and joined the ship in the Clyde from the naval air station at Macrihanish. Dick Janvrin with Scarlett and their wives were out fishing peacefully about five miles from the station that day. It was a lovely, lazy day and a fine, clean flowing burn promising some good eating later, and the trout were rising well. A rather nice little freckle-faced boy on the bridge above watched Janvrin as he cast another hopeful fly.

Suddenly the nice little boy said, 'Are you from the Navy, sir? Because I think you're wanted on the phone.'

It was *Illustrious* summoning her brood.

At Gibraltar Streamline Robertaon watched smugly *Ark Royal* operating her aircraft the 'old-fashioned' way. *Illustrious* arrived there ready and anxious to show her paces. Flying had now reached a high standard and the new radar interception technique showed great promise. Under Captain Boyd's inspired leadership a happy ship's company had been created whose high spirits mounted all the time.

The young pilots were fanatically keen, longing to show their strength. At times they were over-zealous. Bombs would be dropped on shadows or by mistake. One Swordfish returned with all its bombs gone, and Bill Banham asked the pilot:

'Did you sink the sub?'

'What sub?' asked the astonished young man.

'Well, what *did* happen to your anti-submarine bombs?' said Bill with a grin. 'Didn't you know you'd dropped 'em?'

'Er, no, I didn't, actually,' said the pilot awkwardly.

Another Swordfish, which did bring its bombs back, missed all the arrester wires, climbed with its hook still down, caught the barrier and slammed down on to the deck in a spray of blue sparks, flames belching from the exhaust, bombs skidding across the deck in the flood of petrol from the fractured tank. Mercifully nothing caught fire and no one was hurt.

A similar thing happened next day, and the 'goofers' on the bridge island watched with mixed feelings a terrified matelot running as fast as his legs would carry him and looking tearfuly over his shoulder at a large bomb which was chasing him down the flight deck.

Several times high explosive bombs were released from bomb racks when the aircraft were revving up on deck, but luckily the aiming vanes on the bombs did not have sufficient height to set them off. Another careless youngster, sitting happily in his Fulmar down below, pressed the firing button and sprayed the hangar with the contents of eight Browning machine guns. A Swordfish pilot released his torpedo, warhead and firing pistol in place, on to the hangar floor, where it lay quivering and vibrating in a dry run. If one whisker of that pistol had touched anything...

Everybody took these mishaps in their stride, although they thoroughly put the wind up anyone who knew explosives.

As she left Gibraltar in company with *Valiant*, *Calcutta*, *Coventry* and the ships of Force H, Italian spotters picked her up. Captain Boyd swung her into wind and the Fulmars roared off the deck. Soon three Italian machines were burning in the sea.

Then the Swordfish showed what they could do. Bombing up with 250 pound general-purpose bombs they flew out to blast Cagliari in southern Sardinia.

After this Force H left them and they steamed on alone in darkness through the Pantellaria Straits at full speed. The next day mine-mooring wires were removed from the starboard paravane wires. They had steamed straight through a minefield.

Then the fighters were up again, chasing a big force of Italian high level bombers which drenched the carrier's deck with the spray from near misses. Henry Lloyd, the padre, whose action station was at the microphone, was busy broadcasting,

'Our fighters have shot down another bomber.'

Illustrious dealt with shadowers all through that day, and Charles Evans and his boys shot down everything they could catch. The Italians mistook the Fulmars for Spitfires and the R/T crackled with shouts of '*Spittyfurers!*'

They were met south of Sicily by the Battle Fleet and escorted to Atexandria. On the way the new carrier's Swordfish joined with *Eagle*'s in bombing enemy airfields on Rhodes. Hangars and barracks were left blazing and many of the planes which had pestered the Fleet and attacked the oil depots at Haifa were destroyed.

'Hats' was the first operation in the Mediterranean war in which a large fleet had passed from west to east between Sicily and Cape Bon. The opportunity was also taken to pass two convoys with supplies and reinforcements through to beleaguered Malta, under cover of the two fleet sorties from east and west.

Illustrious had arrived. In the weeks that followed she showed her worth. Now the Fleet had eyes. Captain Boyd's new radar gave them instant warning of enemy aircraft and his own planes protected our convoys and searched the sea for submarines.

The Fulmars surpassed themselves again and again. Admiral Cunningham came and told them, 'You young men have altered the course of the war in the Mediterranean.'

They were led by a virtuoso. Charles Evans was an Elizabethan, with his fierce eyes and fiercer red beard, his impatient, springing walk. If you thought of a young Francis Drake when you looked at him, you recalled, too, that Nelson had urged his captains to lay their ships close aboard the enemy. Evans did this with his Fulmars. He had learned to handle fighters in the *Furious* and *Courageous*, learned on the little Flycatchers, with their small 375 horsepower Jaguar engines, the tough and acrobatic machines with no brakes that didn't need wires to get them on the deck. Those were the days when six Flycatchers, each held back by a wire and a slip, would fling themselves at full bore from the flying-off deck beneath the flight deck and climb into a Prince of Wales' feathers formation straight off the bows. 'Always used to duck my head when I shot out of the hangar,' CLG used to say when he remembered those days.

One day Streamline Robertson had to caution him about the excessive use of ammunition by his squadron. Streamline got his answer next day

Tally-ho!' came from Evans over the R/T, then, a minute later:

'One burst – one Wop.'

On the return passage from convoy operations *Illustrious* was frequently detached in strike Italian-held ports on the Libyan coast or airfields in the Dodecanese Islands by moonlight, or to lay mines in the harbours. On 13th September, the Italian army in Libya had begun its advance on Egypt. They had got as far as Sidi Barrani and there had got stuck. On September 17th *Illustrious*' Swordfish attacked Benghazi, which the Italians were using as a base for the supply ships and troopers from Italy which had managed to elude our aircraft and submarines from Malta, since *Eagle*'s bombers had made Tobruk too hot for them. In the light of a full moon, Hale's men dropped mines in the entrance to the harbour, and between them 815 and 819 sank a destroyer and two merchant ships. This sort of attack was *Illustrious*' contribution to the standing operation of punching Mussolini's swelling waistline in Africa, which our destroyers and the brave little gunboat, *Ladybird*, kept up night and day. Royal Air Force and Fleet Air Arm bombers and a handful of submarines from Malta saw to it that many fat ships from Italy never reached Benghazi at all.

One sunny morning the radar warned the Fleet of hostile aircraft. All hands aboard *Illustrious* closed up at action stations. The enemy came closer....

'Aircraft now about forty miles away.... Enemy aircraft now approaching from the starboard quarter... closing the ship very fast... stand by!... Aircraft now eight miles, bearing green 125, 180 degrees....'

Then, after a tense moment. Commander Tuck's voice was heard saying:

'Hands to secure from action stations. The alarm was probably caused by another gaggle of geese.'

He had scarcely finished speaking when there came the tremendous roar and shudder of bombs bursting close. Heavy bombs straddled the ship and she disappeared in a great curtain of white water and boiling spray. One bomb like an enormous dustbin came down wobbling fifty yards off the port bow, blowing a great column of dirty black water and pieces of bomb casing over the flight deck.

Throughout all the fear and tension of battle many of the carrier's men, including her Captain, found peace and strength in a quiet place below decks. The chapel was open always. There, many found the peace of God. It was quiet harbour for them all, away from the fury of the sea – 'the centre of our thoughts,' said Boyd.

On September 30th Admiral Cunningham took part of the Fleet out to cover a convoy to Malta. On the way a force of five Italian battleships was reported near at hand. The C-in-C had with him only two battleships. Thus heavily outnumbered he still hoped for a chance to close the slippery dreadnoughts of Mussolini. But once more they used their greater speed and fled, *ventre-a-terre*, for the shelter of Taranto harbour.

Once again it was deadlock, with the Duce's fat fleet back behind their nets and guns, in harbour, always a potential, never an actual, menace to our ships. This presence of a 'flea in being' at Taranto, like a great pack of hyenas holed up in a cave, kept far too many units of our already shoestring navy tied to the Mediterranean. Cunningham was forced again and again to risk appalling numerical odds because, if the Italian Fleet *could* be caught and destroyed, the whole great inland sea could be opened again from west to east. Our forces, particularly Wavell's army in Africa, and the 'unsinkable aircraft-carrier' of Malta, could then be rapidly reinforced and the Italians firmly dealt with for good and all. This desire was very strong in Mr Churchill's mind.

On September 8th he signalled to Admiral Cunningham;

'I congratulate you upon the success of the recent operation in the Eastern and Central Mediterranean, and upon the accession to your fleet of two of our finest units, with other valuable vessels. I hope you will find it possible to review the naval situation in the light of the experience gained during "Hats" and the arrival of *Illustrious* and *Valiant*. Not only the paper strength of the Italian Navy, but also the degree of resistance which they may be inclined to offer, should be measured. It is of high importance to strike the Italians this autumn, because as time passes the Germans will be more likely to lay strong hands upon the Italian war machine, and then the picture will be very different.

Our battleships could not catch the fast *Littorios*, *Cavours* and *Duilios* at sea. There was only one answer. We must smash them in harbour. A cutting-out expedition in the old tradition was called for. Drake and Nelson had done it, although Taranto could not be attacked with ships, and land-based bombers, even if we had had enough, would have found the Italians waiting for them behind their massed guns.

But now *Illustrious* was here, and with her was Lumley Lyster and the nucleus of his torpedo droppers from the *Glorious*.

Dudley Pound had meant to use the *Glorious* squadron in 1938 if war had come then. He had foreseen the present need when he asked Lyster to be ready to send his Swordfish against the Italian Fleet in harbour. Now Pound was at the Admiralty and Lyster was back in the Mediterranean with a brand-new carrier and the core of that hard-thrusting group from *Glorious* who had practised this very form of attack so thoroughly under his command. The answer to a gun-shy enemy was the torpedo bomber.

Taranto was watched constantly by RAF reconnaissance machines from

Malta which photographed ships in the harbour and defences. Simultaneously the Swordfish crews in *Illustrious* and *Eagle* began intensified night-flying training.

There were many who said it could not be done, that Lyster was throwing away his career. And it was easy for them to talk, for nothing like this, on such a scale and with stakes so high, had ever been done before.

But it seemed the only way to knock out the Italians, and Lyster and Boyd were at last given October 21st, Trafalgar Day, to do it.

At last the time came when the aircrews and their machines were ready. Then the luck of *Illustrious* broke down.

As they were fitting a long-range tank into one of her Swordfish, one of the batteries short-circuited, a spark caught a petrol drip from the tank, which had not been properly emptied, and soon there was a raging fire in the hangar.

When the flames had been got under control, two Swordfish lay completely gutted and five others damaged and encrusted with the salt water which had been poured on them. Taranto was postponed for ten days. The squadron personnel turned to and worked without rest to bring the damaged machines to readiness again. Salt-caked radios were put out in the sun to dry and every part of each machine was checked and made good.

As an immediate alternative to Taranto, Cunningham took his battleships to sea again in the hope of enticing the Italians to battle, at the same time covering another convoy to Malta. They saw nothing of the enemy's main fleet, but on the way back, escorting an east-bound convoy, the cruiser *Ajax* sighted two Italian destroyers by moonlight and attacked them. One was left burning and was sunk next morning by the *York*, and the other blew up.

Meanwhile, *Illustrious* and *Eagle* had been detached from the Fleet for a raid on the Dodecanese.

They slipped through the Matapan Channel, bombed hangars, workshops and fuel tanks on Leros at dawn, then raced back east of Crete to join the Fleet. But they had stirred up trouble.

As darkness fell on a bright moonlight night the Fleet was steering southwards towards Alexandria but was still within air striking distance of the enemy at Rhodes. It seemed an ideal sight for an enemy air attack.

About seven miles astern of *Illustrious* was the cruiser *Newcastle*. Suddenly, during the first watch, she signalled:

'Torpedoed!'

Almost simultaneously a report came up from the radar room:

'Formation of enemy aircraft approaching about seven miles... now five miles...'

Commander Tuck was on watch and instantly pressed the alarm rattlers. In a matter of seconds the Captain was on the bridge and Tuck leapt down the ladders to his action station in the lower conning-tower on the main deck. He found Commander (E) and the Master-at-Arms already in the damage control headquarters and the damage control parties closing up. All hands below sat down clear of obstructions. If a torpedo hit, it would be better to be sitting down already than to be blown down.

In the lower conning-tower they could hear Toswill, the Navigator, repeating the Captain's orders – 'Emergency turn to starboard' or 'Starboard twenty'.

At that instant all the pom-poms in the ship opened fire, giving an all-round curtain of fire at eighty feet from bow to stern on either side, the thumping of the guns bring punctuated by the helm orders from the bridge.

Then, all of a sudden, the noise ceased and there was complete silence. The attack was over. The Fleet turned to rejoin the damaged *Newcastle*, whose bows were hanging off, and slowly, next day, they escorted her back to Alexandria, with *Orion* towing the crippled cruiser stern-first and finding it very hard going, as *Newcastle*'s stern, hanging deep in the water, had a will of its own and acted as a rudimentary rudder.

At three o'clock on the morning of October 28, Italy sent an ultimatum to Greece demanding the occupation of Crete, Corfu, Salonika and other strategic points. Greece refused these demands and went to war.

This at once put an even heavier burden upon the already straining back of the Royal Navy. We now had an ally in the Mediterranean – but our ships would have to defend her. Convoys would have to be escorted through the Aegean, running the gauntlet of the Dodecanese, defences would have to be provided for Crete, and Malta supplied as usual. And if this situation were not bad enough, there was still an Italian 'fleet in being', with a whole new display of tempting targets laid out in Greek waters. The attack on Taranto was more urgent than ever.

Illustrious and *Eagle* were scheduled to carry it out on the 31st. But again there was a hitch. There would be no moon that night, so the attack relied upon flares. At the last moment it was decided that the flare droppers had had insufficient practice.

Once again the attack was called off. It was finally planned for the night of November 11th, Armistice Day. The aircrews, fretted and hoped fervently that nothing would stop them this time.

The Taranto attack was to fit into an overall plan for a combined operation covering convoy movements to Greece, Crete and Malta, and designated MB.8, of which part was formed by Operation *Coat*, a movement of warship reinforcements to the Fleet, part by Operation *Crack*, an attack by *Ark Royal* from Force H upon Cagliari in Sardinia to cover Operation *Coat*, and part by Operation *Judgement*, the attack on the Italian Battle Fleet in Taranto.

Then a bad blow struck the enterprise. Two days before the Fleet was due to sail from Alexandria, *Eagle's* petrol system, badly shaken by many near misses, broke down and she had to drop out. But *Illustrious* borrowed five of her aircrews and their machines, now that she would have to go it alone, so the old veteran would be represented after all.

The Fulmar flown to Malta on the morning of the 11th to collect the latest photographs of Taranto harbour returned to *Illustrious* with those taken the day before. Lyster and his officers studied the photographs closely.

They saw the familiar shape of the great anchorage – two adjoining harbours shaped like a cottage loaf, the big one, Mar Grande, opening on the sea through breakwaters lined with anti-aircraft guns and, on its landward side, admitting through a narrow channel to the smaller, inner harbour, Mar Piccolo.

First, they looked for ships. There were plenty there. Sitting fat and smug in the outer harbour lay the unmistakable shapes of five battleships, two of the new Littorio Class and three of the recently reconstructed Cavour and Duilio Class, and three cruisers. In the inner harbour were cruisers and destroyers.

The five battleships represented five-sixths of the total Italian battleship strength. This was the main target.

The photographs were examined with stereoscopic glasses. They noted the position of tbe anti-torpedo nets and noticed something else which worried them. Along the seaward side of the Diga di Tarantola, a long mole which stuck out inside the outer harbour like a protecting arm round that side of the battleship group that was not protected by nets or the land, stretched a number of tiny white dots – balloons. Balloon defences also lined the shore and the far side of the nets and the whole anchorage was ringed with anti-aircraft guns.

It was decided to attack in two waves. As the balloons and nets seriously restricted suitable torpedo-dropping positions, only half of each wave would carry torpedoes. The others would carry bombs, or bombs and flares. The torpedo carriers were to attack the battleships in the outer harbour and, as a diversion, for bombers were to carry out a synchronised attack on cruisers and destroyers alongside the quay and in the inner harbour.

Finally, the Mediterranean Fleet, with *Illustrious*, left Alexandria on November 6th. MB.8 – and Taranto – was on. This was it.

On the 8th seven Italian SM.79's attacked the Fleet. Charles Evans and two of his pilots scrambled, made a view, gave a laconic 'tally-ho!' and shot down two of the bombers, driving the rest away.

'Very good show, Charles!' said Captain Boyd, when the fighter leader returned.

'Oh, I didn't do anything, sir,' said CLG, raising his fierce eyebrows. 'My other two chaps shot them down.'

'I hear you're to be congratulated,' said Boyd to the other two fighter pilots when they appeared.'

'It wasn't us, sir,' said the two of them, almost in unison. 'The CO shot them down.'

Next day a nosey Cant 506 B shadower put in an appearance, and his brief candle was promptly snuffed out by Evans.

All seemed set. But still bad luck dogged the striking force. Patrolling Swordfish from the carrier were suddenly struck by a plague of engine failures, due to contaminated petrol.

In one of these machines Going, of Hale's squadron, was out on a reconnaissance flight with a rather inexperienced young pilot. Suddenly, when they were twenty miles from the Fleet, the engine cut out.

'I'm afraid the engine's stopped,' said the pilot.

'I wondered what the deathly 'ush was,' said Going.

"What do I do now?' asked the pilot.

Going held back a whole flood of witty answers.

'Well, if I were you, old boy, I should try gliding in the vague direction of the Fleet – over there!' he said.

Then they hit the sea. The pilot pulled the special toggle in the centre section, releasing the plane's rubber dinghy. Going unhooked his observer's 'anti-cavorting' chain and executed a smart dive over the centre section. Around them he saw several flame floats released from the plane. In the distance he made out the grey shapes of *Gloucester* and *York* heading towards the Fleet to rejoin. He swam to one of the flame floats and lit it.

Gloucester saw the tiny fire, altered course and picked up pilot, observer and air gunner. Aboard the cruiser they dried off and had a good hot breakfast, over which Going chatted to Tubby Lane, the pilot of *Gloucester*'s Walrus amphibian. Perhaps the thought of the Walrus prompted him, but anyway he began to think that perhaps he ought to go and have a word with, the Captain about getting back to *Illustrious*. The others be knew would be wanted urgently next morning for anti-submarine patrols as the aircrews going to Taranto that night would have to be counted out for such duties. Besides, he was scheduled for Taranto himself and rather wanted to go....

'I think it's important we should get back, sir,' he said to Captain Morse. Eventually the Captain was persuaded to send a signal to the C-in-C asking permission for the *Illustrious* men to be returned to their ship. Permission was granted, they all piled aboard Tubby Lane's Walrus and were catapulted off. Half an hour later, about quarter past two, the Walrus clanked and grunted her way on to *Illustrious'* flight deck and deposited her wayward sons. Going immediately got together with Clifford, his regular pilot, collected a new chart board and equipment, and made ready for Taranto.

In the afternoon the RAF reported that a sixth battleship had entered Taranto harbour. The whole bag was there now.

Mussolini had put all his eggs in one basket.

Tension mounted aboard, from the Admiral down to the youngest boy seaman. There was a great sweat and bustle on in the hangar, where men were still working on the machines that were to go that night. The men who were to go felt their excitement rise as the hours went by. To Hale and the old *Glorious* men this moment that drew inexorably on was the consummation they had worked so hard to achieve, that some of their best friends had died for in the far-off days of that uneasy peace. All knew this approaching climax for what it was – the moment of truth for the Fleet Air Arm. Taranto was the anvil upon which their branch would be shaped or broken.

At six o'clock the moment of final decision came. The Rear-Admiral, Aircraft Carriers, in the *Illustrious*, supported by the Third Cruiser Squadron and four destroyers, was detached to proceed in execution of previous orders.

'Good luck,' signalled the Commander-in-Chief, as they parted company with the Fleet, 'to your lads in their enterprise.'

Then they were on their own.

The carrier and her escort were to be in a position at eight o'clock forty miles, 270 degrees, from Kabbo Point, Cephalonia, and fly off at that hour the first group of twelve aircraft. The second group of aircraft were to be launched an hour later from the same position.

The first attack was to be made about a quarter to eleven and the second at a quarter to midnight. The aircraft were to land on the carrier again at a point twenty miles, 270 degrees, from Point Kabbo. There were many who feared that the latter was an academic provision.

By eight o'clock, on schedule, *Illustrious* reached the flying-off position, one hundred and seventy miles from Taranto.

By now the aircraft had been finally readied, electrics, rigging, machine-guns, engines checked and counter-checked. Bombs and torpedoes were brought up from the bowels of the ship and transferred to the parked aircraft. The RAF sergeant rigger, who had been working flat-out for thirty-six hours, reported the last aircraft ready to Lieutenant-Commander Williamson, and the ranging of aircraft on the flight deck began about seven o'clock. Then pilots and observers of Williamson's first wave of twelve Swordfish mustered in the ready room for final briefing.

The squadron was to fly in formation to the target area and make a detour to the north of the harbour, separating for their different roles in the attack, the bombers to attack the cruisers and destroyers, the flare droppers to illuminate the battleships from behind while the torpedo droppers swept in low over the harbour, making their own way through the balloon defences and carrying out individual attacks on the battleships. Wireless silence was to be maintained, the squadron commander to make one signal only – 'Attack completed'.

It was an almost windless night with detached cloud obscuring the moon. At eleven thirty *Illustrious* was steaming hard to provide enough wind over the flight deck for the Swordfish heavily laden with torpedoes or bombs and the extra fuel tanks which had displaced the air gunners in their rear cockpits.

Commander Tuck stood on the flight deck, watching the pilots and observers climb into their cockpits and wishing them all good luck.

Everything was ready now. The Swordfish were manned and warmed up, their propellers ticking lazily over. Each machine was reported correct.

Zero hour. The countersunk lights on the flight deck were switched on – two tramlines of light swaying ahead in the darkness between which each machine must steer to get off safely.

They were ready to go. Captain Boyd swung the ship into wind. A tearing gale of wind began to rush over the bows and down the flight deck.

Somewhere in the black outline of the bridge island a green light blinked. It was Streamline's torch.

Fly off!

Immediately wheel chocks were whipped from under Williamson's wheels and he was torched off. The dark, bulky shape roared down the deck, left the bows and fell away, so that everyone could feel Williamson's physical effort to keep the heavily laden Swordfish airborne.

Then he gained height and climbed up into the darkness. After him, one by one down the deck, came the others of his squadron at close intervals, leaping forward under full throttle and lifting off the carrier's deck on the great flood of the wind. The padre, as usual, kept up a running commentary over the ship's loud-speakers to the men closed up at defence stations. Streamline Robertson leaned over the bridge and stared into the darkness. Douglas Russell was already starting to range up Hale's squadron of the second wave. Down in the ready room George Beale briefed the second batch of pilots and observers in his quiet and thorough way.

The first wave were all in the air now. Eight miles from the carrier they formed up on Williamson's aircraft, men set course for Taranto, a hundred and seventy miles away across a black sea spangled fitfully now and then with moonlight.

Soon it was the turn of the second wave to go. Hale led them off the deck and they climbed to form up, then turned for Taranto and disappeared in the night, the blessing of two great ships going with them. The old Fleet Air Arm and the new went out together.

But they left one machine behind them on the deck. Clifford and Going had been ranged farthest aft, last in the second range along the port side. As the Swordfish in the opposite line to starboard wheeled out and on to the centre line, its wing-tip caught Clifford's wing, tearing the fabric and breaking several ribs inside it.

It looked like finish for them. The Swordfish, still loaded with its bombs, was struck down into the hangar.

But they did not give up. While Clifford rounded up weary mechanics down in the hanger and set them to work to repair the damage. Going, his hair still wet from the ducking of that morning, rushed up to the Air Intelligence Office where David Pollock was talking to the US Navy liaison officer attached to *Illustrious*. Going began cursing his luck and saying that they must go to Taranto.

'Well, boy,' said the American, 'if you feel that way about it, why the hell don't you go and tell your Captain?'

It wasn't orthodox Royal Navy practice but Going took his advice and went straight up to see Captain Boyd on the bridge.

'Sir,' he said, 'we must go to Taranto.'

'But my dear fellow,' said Boyd, 'you've smashed your bleeding aircraft.'

'We can repair the damage in ten minutes if you'll let us go, sir. I know we can catch up with the others.'

In the face of such determination the Captain had to agree. He sent Going and Clifford up to Admiral Lyster's bridge to get his permission, where they appeared, as the Admiral thought, looking like two terriers who had been ratting. Their machine was repaired. Could they go to Taranto?

'Well, you're flying the bloody aircraft,' said Lyster. 'All right, off you go!'

So, thirty minutes after the others had gone, Swordfish L5F was torched off and launched into the empty night, 'in view', as the official report said later, 'of the keenness of the crew and their confidence in reaching the others.'

They had been gone less than an hour when those aboard *Illustrious* heard the drone of an aircraft. Then a red Very light burst in the sky. *Illustrious* and the cruiser *Berwick* opened fire. The aircraft immediately fired a two-star indication light and they knew it was one of the Swordfish.

Fifteen minutes later two very disgusted young men. Lieutenants Marford and Green, were sitting in the wardroom. When they were well on course their external overload tank had fallen off, leaving loose fittings banging against the fuselage and making a nuisance of themselves. There was nothing to do but return to the carrier.

After this there were no more alarms. *Illustrious* continued on her reverse course and everyone settled down as much as their excitement would allow to wait far the signal from the first wave.

Commander Tuck went down to the wardroom and asked what arrangements were in hand to feed the aircrews on thier return.

He found that an enormous eggs-and-bacon feast had been laid on.

'And look at this, sir,' said the messman proudly. It was a big iced 'Greetings' cake which be had prepared for the returning fliers....

...Aboard the *Littorio* there was no thought of preparation. The young *guardia marina* on watch hitched up his bright blue sash and listened enviously to the singing coming up from the mess decks below. The men were in good spirits. They had turned out that morning dripping and cursing at the thought of a day's gunnery exercises, and sweated the morning watch away unrigging the anti-torpedo nets that swaddled the ships. Then the Admiral had called off the exercise. Their was a buzz that the British Fleet was at sea.

They hadn't bothered to rig the nets again.

The whole of Taranto was on edge that night. Before eight an alert had been given ashore, following a report of aircraft coming from the coast south-east of the Gulf. A few minutes later the alarm went. The suspicious noises received from positions nearest the ring of observation posts had been confirmed.

On board the ships the crews closed up at action stations, but half an hour later the all-clear sounded.

At nine o'clock a fresh alert was signalled from the Fortress HQ, followed by the alarm five minutes later. Then the noises died away and the all-clear came at nine-thirty.

The noise of aircraft was picked up again at twenty-five past ten and HQ gave the alert once more. Gradually the sound faded, but, just before it died altogether the alarm was sounded on fresh noises being picked up inwards the south and south-east. The defences were now thoroughly rattled and the ack-ack batteries in the San Vito zone commenced, barrage fire in the direction of the aircraft noises.

The noise that had died away into the night was an RAF Sunderland of 228 Squadron from Malta.

The second batch of noises, which now became a swelling cadenza of sound, was the first wave from *Illustrious*, forty miles away and closing fast...

At ten fifty-two, Scarlett, in the back seat of Williamson's leading Swordfish, looked up and said briefly:

'There's Taranto.'

They were the first words he had spoken during the whole trip, but even he was stirred to speech by the sight of the great Brock's benefit glaring ahead of them on the skyline. The night sky was bright with tracer and bursting shells.

Four minutes later Janvrin and the others detailed to drop flares were detached to drop them along the eastern shore of the harbour. Janvrin made two or three runs, saw that the job was done, then told Kiggell, the pilot, who took them off to find a target for their bombs.

An Italian report said later: 'Shortly before each attack a series of five or six or more brilliant flashes were dropped by parachute and landed in a chain along the shore between San Vito and Torre d'Ayala, in the direction of south to north at a height of six hundred and fifty feet. The illumination of the flares lasted between three and four minutes, these forming a zone of intense light to the eastward of the battleships, whose hulls were clearly outlined....'

Right at that stark silhouette Williamson led his torpedo droppers, straight for the 'zone of intense light'.

Williamson and Scarlett saw nothing of the thick balloon barrage they had been especially warned about, passing clear through the forest of cables without even taking avoiding action.

They came in low over San Pietro island and the outer break-water, and in seconds were in the thick of things. The long, curling fingers of the tracers reached up for them, the glowing red of the incendiary bullets, the blue of the explosive, and the armour-piercing, the ones they could not see....

He dropped down to attack level, the sheen of the water jazzing with the reflection of flame and bursting shells. Seeing the long shape of a Cavour, rippling along her decks with anti-aircraft fire, he made straight for her. It would be the first time he or anyone else there had ever dropped a torpedo at night in action.

Theory ruled that a torpedo should be released at a hundred and fifty feet. But from that height the pilots knew that any one of a dozen things would go wrong and ruin the attack, so Williamson had determined to go down to thirty feet before dropping.

When he did drop the torpedo he felt a great splash of water, so he must have been even lower.

There was no time to see if he had hit. He concentrated all his energy on getting clear of the barrage. Just as he was crossing the floating dock that lay on the far side of the battleships his engine stopped, hit by fire from below, and they crashed into the sea between the dock and a group of destroyers.

Meanwhile, the others were making their attacks. Sparke and Macauley in the two other planes of the first sub-flight, led in by Williamson, flattened out at thirty feet and swept in over the breakwater. They saw the floating dock to starboard, picked out the shape of a Cavour ahead, and dropped their torpedoes.

Kemp in the fourth machine steered straight for the northern *Littorio*. As he dropped his torpedo there was time for Bailey, his observer, to notice that it was on target and running correctly.

Maund, in the fifth torpedo dropper, made through heavy shell-fire for the southerly *Littorio*, made an accurate drop and doubled back.

Swayne and Buscall in the sixth torpedo dropper had lost the rest of the squadron shortly after leaving *Illustrious* and had, arrived a quarter of an hour before the others. Waiting until he saw the first flare light up, Swayne came in, picked up the southern *Littorio* ahead and went right in to four hundred yards before dropping his torpedo. As he passed over the battleship they saw a column of smoke shoot up abaft the funnels.

At the same time the rest of the strike were pressing home their bombing attacks on the ships in the inner harbour and anything they could find nearby.

Then, less than an hour later. Hale brought the second wave to. He had eight machines with him, with Clifford and Going in L5F some way behind.

These two had a long, three-hour flight from the ship when, seventy miles from the target, they saw the fiery aftermath of the first attack in the sky, which was bright as day with the pyrotechnics of starshell and tracer.

Coming in from the opposite direction to the first wave they attacked.

Hale saw the ships low on the water, well lit up by the moon, with the cruisers on the right. He had already decided on the northerly of the two *Littorios* and kept an eye on it on the way down to attack level.

They went down in line astern to forty feet, each pilot watching the blue formation lights of the plane ahead. Hale smelt the acrid fumes of shell bursts as they dived. Then they flattened out and each attacked independently.

A quarter of a mile to go. Hale got the upper deck of his target in line with the horizon. *Mustn't skid sideways. Funny, no searchlights – they could have dazzled us at four hundred yards...That's about it...Bit closer.... Now!* The plane jumped as the torpedo fell away....

Aboard *Illustrious*, nearly two hundred miles away off the dark coast of Cephalonia, they had waited in vain for Williamson's signal. But Williamson was now sipping rum in the wardroom of the Italian destroyer that had shot him down. The Italians told him he had hit his target.

They were all anxious for the first wave. Then, after a dreadful, tense lifetime of waiting and wondering, the signal came from the second strike:

'Attack completed!'

The first they knew of the fate of the first attack was the sudden appearance of two aircraft switching on their dimmed navigation lights overhead. When three or four machines had gathered and rendezvoused, *Illustrious* turned to land them on.

The Swordfish came over the stern silently, like woodcock in flight, heading one after the other into the softly shaded stern lights like great grey shadows, with Douglas Russel coaxing them down to the deck with outstretched, dimly illuminated bats.

All heads craned over the bridge watching the undercarriages. There were no torpedoes there.

Observers jumped down and dashed across the deck to the ready room, clearly beside themselves with excitement. There George Beale took them quietly in hand, stopping the excited babble of conversation and making them sit silently to write up their attack report form independently.

Tuck stood near them trying to piece together these first impressions of what they had achieved.

Captain Boyd came in.

'Well, Ging,' he said to one of the youngsters, 'did you have a good evening?'

'Yes, sir.'

'Did you fait anything?'

'Yes, sir, I hit a battleship.'

'How do you know?'

'I went back to have a look, sir.'

Other pilots had done the same thing.

'Oh, I flew back through the same hole,' said one.

'Did you get shot at much?' another was asked.

'Oh, there was bags of stuff coming up, you know, but nothing personal until I flew across the bows of a cruiser and she let off her eight-inch at me,' he said.

One by one the Swordfish came back. As each one landed everybody's heart rose a little higher. Most of the men were back now, and from the look of things they seemed to have done pretty well.

But it was not until Clifford and Going landed again, some time after the others, that Lyster and Boyd began to get a reasonably coherent picture.

It appeared that they had dived on a cruiser and returned to make a second run because they were uncertain as to whether their bombs had left the aircraft, with Going sticking his head over the side of the cockpit taking a good took at the state of affairs below.

He reported seeing two ships listing and one down by the bows, with others obviously damaged.

But they all kept their fingers crossed until, two days later, RAF photographs showed the *Littorio* lying with a heavy list and her fo'c'sfe awash, one *Cavour* with her stern under water as far as the after turret, and one *Duilio* beached and abandoned. There were two cruisers lying in a wide pool of oil, bleeding like mortally wounded pigs, and two fleet auxiliaries lying with their sterns under water. The seaplane base and the oil storage depot, had obviously been badly damaged.

It was only then that they realised they had won a famous victory.

CHAPTER THREE

THE FIGHT FOR LIFE

'Come on, we've got to get ready,' said the pilot.

...What the hell for?' asked the observer.

'We're going to Taranto again tonight' said the other.

'What – *again!* My God! They only asked the Light Brigade to do it once!'

A second attack *had* been scheduled but bad weather cancelled it and *Illustrious* rejoined the Fleet at Alexandria. Cuimingham signalled:

'*Illustrious*. Manoeuvre well executed.'

They had lost two Swordfish in the attack and one aircrew from the *Eagle*, but these were small losses to balance against the enormous gain.

At six o'clock on 12th November people at home in England switched on their radios and heard,

'...The Italians today admit a raid on their naval base at Taranto, in southern Italy. They say that only one ship was extensively damaged....'

Taranto had freed the Mediterranean for the British Fleet. Now those vital convoys could come in from the west, bringing food, ammunition and Hurricanes to Malta, and guns and troops to General Wavell in the desert.

On December 7 Wavell struck back hard at the Italian army in North

Africa and immediately began to drive it back in disorder. In Greece, too, the Italians were being stampeded by a fierce Greek counter-offensive.

All this the men of *Illustrious* had helped to bring about. Unfortunately for them, in doing so they had helped to force a more serious issue as well.

They had brought the Germans to the Mediterranean. The Swordfish had gone to Taranto. Now the *Stukas* had come to Sicily.

It was a direct result of Mussolini's total failure. When Hitler's Tenth Air Corps veterans left the snows of Norway for sunny Sicily it was the sign of a strategic victory which was to have disastrous effects in the future upon the Axis war effort. However, for the present it was going to mean hell on earth for the victors. They had forced the Germans to move one hundred and fifty Heinkels and Junkers 88's, a hundred and fifty *Stukas* and fifty Messerschmitts from Norway, Denmark, Holland, Belgium and France to Sicily.

And they brought the whole force of it down, literally, upon their own heads.

General Geissler, the tough, aggressive commanding officer of the Tenth Air Corps, knew well his priorities. He had three hundred bombers including some of the best anti-shipping units in the world. Malta was their target.

But first of all – *Illustrious*.

Just after lunchtime on the 10th January, the gunners on Malta shaded their eyes and watched three low-wing fighters sweep in at high speed from the direction of Sicily. At first sight they looked like Hurricanes, but as they came closer those who knew their aircraft recognised them as Fulmars, the navy fighters that had been doing such finework in recent months. The three fighters circled Valetta and went in to land at Hal Far airfield!

Where had they come from? Even before the Fulmars touched down the answer came in the form of a signal sent urgently to all the anti-aircraft gun-sites on the island:

'Stand by. Aircraft carrier *Illustrious* damaged – putting into Grand Harbour.'

The Fulmars were Charles Evans' men. Somewhere away to the north-west of Malta the Axis was revenging itself for Taranto. The ship that had hurt them so badly was fighting for her life.

Illustrious had known all about those Heinkels and Junkers. Her reconnaissance machines had reported them – lying in hundreds at Catania and Comiso. In the first light of dawn on January 10th she found herself steaming west through the Pantellaria Straits, on her way to pick up a convoy. Previous runs of this kind had been done at night, but now day brighter and brighter over the mastheads of the British ships.

Pantellaria loomed up to starboard. The Italians were said to have fifteen-inch guns ashore there. If they had, they did not choose to use them that morning. The ships drew on deeper and deeper into the channel.

Reconnaissance and anti-submarine patrols were up as unual from the carrier, and a patrol of Fulmars was overhead: a force of Swordfish, armed with bombs had been flown off to attack, enemy shipping.

The bombers were in two sub-flights, one led by Hale, and one by Jago, the new CO of 815 Squadron.

Jago, another old *Glorious* pilot, had been ghd to come to *Illustrious*. He had come out to the Mediterranean in the *Valiant,* and had watched with some frustration all the way out the constant air activity aboard the carrier. Going first to Dekheila airfield in Egypt as spare CO, he had been sent hurriedly to the new base at Suda Bay in Crete when Greece came into the war. The Navy gave him a five-pound note and told him he had four days to build an airfield as close to Suda as possible. He had built his airfield, with the aid of the local Imperial Airways agent and a blank cheque from the British Naval Attaché at Athens, and had returned to Alexandria just in time to go to *Illustrious* in place of Williamson, captured at Taranto.

They made a good start that morning. Reece had reported an Italian convoy nearby. It was a lovely day and they saw the convoy clearly. There were three merchantmen, one destroyer and a small escort vessel. Jago put his nose down and attacked the lead ship. He saw a bomb go straight down the open for'd hatchway. They sank the second, a large, liner, as well, and despatched the third, all in a matter of minutes. The escorts did not open fire until the Swordfish were well out of range, and making for *Illustrious*. On their way back Jago flew over the bows of an Italian destroyer badly shot up by the cruiser *Bonaventure* earlier in the day. Then they picked up the carrier and landed on. There seemed to be plenty of work to be done that day. Jago stood by in the hangar, waiting to lead off another strike.

He was still in the hangar at twelve o'clock. The ship's company had been closed up at action stations all night and everybody was tired, especially the green-new pom-pom gunners who had replaced twenty-one of the old guns' crews transferred at Alexandria for shore training.

Six Fulmars were up and steering east when the ship's radar reported several large groups of hostile aircraft closing rapidly.

Illustrious began to make a leg north from the Fleet to get sea room to fly off more fighters ranged up on deck and land on the other six, which were now running out of fuel.

At ten minutes past twelve two Italian torpedo bombers came in to try, their luck. They approached low to starboard, almost touching the water as they lumbered towards the carrier. All guns on the starboard side opened fire. At four hundred yards the bombers dropped their torpedoes. Captain Boyd altered course sharply to starboard and they missed. The bombers got away unscathed. Bill Banham called up to Anstice, the commissioned gunner in charge of S2 pom-pom.

'Hi, Annie, what's up, missing a sitter like that?'

'Come up and try and shoot the bastards down yourself!' shouted Anstice.

Now the carrier headed into wind and began to launch the fresh Fulmars. Dick Janvrin had joined Jago in the hangar and they were pacing up and down, weighing the chances of another strike.

'I think I'll go and get a spot of lunch while I can,' said Jago. 'Coming?'

'No, thanks,' said Janvrin. 'I've just had mine.'

'Righto. See you later.'

Jago went below. He had just begun his lunch when they heard the guns start up again. He left his food and rushed back to the hangar.

Douglas Russell had just managed to get most of the relieving Fulmars airborne when a large force of *Stukas* peeled off overhead and screamed down straight for the ship. In fact the last fighter scrambled through the wild spray of near misses. The Fulmars climbed all out but they were slow climbers at best. It was up to Bill Acworth's guns.

The *Stukas* came in from three bearings, port and starboard bows and starboard quarter, all at the same time. Bill Banham watched them, diving in groups of three from each direction, dove-tailed neatly together, clover-leaf fashion. Down they hurled through the 4.5 barrage and into the pom-pom screen.'

Nothing could stop them. In a terrifying crescendo of crashing sound. *Illustrious* disappeared in spray and smoke. All was bursting bombs, bursting shells, the racket of the guns and the roar and scream of aircraft.

They knocked the broadcasting system out of action and shattered the radar. A bomb hit P1 pom-pom on the port side for'd, smashing the gun, killing two of its crew as it passed through the gun platform and exploded on hitting the water, sending jagged pieces flying upwards to kill and wound more men.

The bombers that came in from the starboard bow hit S2 pom-pom and destroyed it and all its crew. This same bomb killed three men at S1 pom-pom below and injured many in the ammunition supply parties.

Another heavy bomb fell directly into the after-lift well when the after lift was halfway down. On the lift was a Fulmar with its young midshipman pilot in the cockpit.

Jago, in the hangar, heard a great crash aft. The Fulmar on the lift had been obliterated and the lift itself thrown up end on.

Aircraft at that end of the hangar started to burn. Heavy chunks of metal from the bomb flew in all directions through the walls of the lift well and into the gun bays of the after turrets.

All eight 4.5-inch guns located after were knocked out and their crews killed or injured.

In the hangar fire started to get a hold among the aircraft.

Janvrin, climbing on to a Swordfiah to get a first-aid kit out of the machine, suddenly felt the whole aircraft jump into the air and hurl sideways. He felt nothing himself, but when his feet touched the deck his legs gave under him and he realised he had been hit.

Tuck was down on the main deck with the central damage control parties when he felt the heavy shock aft. He immediately ran with Gutteridge, the shipwright, and the bosun along the main deck to the scene of the explosion. There he found the lift well shattered and men fighting the fires which had developed.

Then the bomb burst for'd on P1 pom-pom. Damage Control HQ reported all the damage to Captain Boyd on the bridge, who was taking rapid avoiding, action with his eye on the diving *Stukas*.

Pilots and observers were helping to fight the fires. Going had been rubber-necking up on the starboard catwalk when blast blew his cap off. Hastening below to see what he could do he found the after flat in darkness. He went to his cabin, collected his torch and on making his way further aft discovered that the after damage control officer had been killed. He decided to remain below and take his place.

Up on the flight deck a few of the hands were rigging fire hoses. Bill Acworth and Bill Banham lent them a hand. Through the flames and smoke shooting up from the after lift they saw a stoker petty officer staggering under the weight of an officer's body.

'Well done,' said Acworth quietly.

S2 pom-pom was a blackened, twisted wreck. Poor old Annie. All that remained was a heap of smouldering clothes and a leg in a seaboot. Men at S1 pom-pom were removing the remains of their oppos. In the middle of the flight deck lay the torso of a man. Captain Boyd noticed it from the bridge, caught the eye of the chief bosun's mate, who was heaving on a hose with Bill Banham, and nodded. The petty officer picked up the bloody object and heaved it overboard.

The padre came up. 'Have a biscuit,' he said, calmly holding out a big paper bag. Then the screech of the warning telephones started again as another wave of bombers screamed down at the ship.

High-level bombers came over this time as welll. Once again the ship lurched and staggered as bombs fell all around her. Noise between decks was terrifying, like a thousand tube trains roaring out of the tunnel. A bomb smashed, through the flight deck and through the boys' mess deck. Passing out of the ship's side it hit the water and exploded. White hot metal shot in all directions, holing the ship in many places above and below the waterline and causing bad flooding in the unamoured for'd section. Blast from the same bomb smashed aircraft in the hangar and punched the for'd lift, upwards into an arch. Wind rusted immediately into the hangar through this arch, and fanned the fires there into a great blaze. Flame and smoke poured from the after-lift well.

Jago had dashed into a spraying room at the side of the hangar to get the sprayers working. When he got back into the hangar it was a ghastly shambles. Dead and badly wounded men lay on the deck, some hit by pieces of steel from the hangar fire screens which had shattered to pieces and flung sharp slivers like scythe blades through the hangar. He saw an officer he knew looking straight at him. The man had no top to his head. He immediately had all access doors to the hangar closed and got the sprayers going. Ammunition was exploding all over the hangar and planes were burning. Down one side of the hangar were six Swordfish with depth-charges attached, and another six armed with torpedoes.

'Don't worry,' said the Gunner(T), 'they won't cook off.'

Streamline Robertson appeared in the hangar. He saw four Fulmars, one in each corner of the after sub-hangar, on fire, and noticed that although many of the Swordfish were shattered and burning, their torpedoes were still intact. More than anything else he felt furiously angry that the Nazis were spoiling the ship.

The flight deck became in places laminated with the heat and too hot to walk on. When water was turned on from the hoses, clouds of steam arose to mingle with the smoke and flame pouring up from the lift well and the holes in the deck. Those guns still intact kept firing.

Then there was a blinding, staggering crash and a great thousand-pounder struck the flight deck right on the centre line.

It burst through the armoured deck and the hangar deck below, hit the after ammunition conveyer and exploded, killing and badly wounding everybody in the wardroom flat. All the officers taking a hasty meal in the wardroom were wiped out. The whole after part of the ship went dark and dead. The fire took hold everywhere and raged through the torn and shattered compartments where men lay trapped. A smashed petrol pipe sprayed streams of liquid flame through the dark, smoke-filled passages.

Bill Banham found that the after bulkhead door was partially open. Peering into the wardrom flat through the thick, acrid haze, he saw the flare from a burning petrol pipe roaring like a huge blowlamp. Ammunition near the shattered conveyer started to go up. Flame suddenly appeared through the openings in the conveyor.

Bill flashed his torch round the shattered keyboard flat. The secondary light lamps had gone, the magazine light boxes, junction and distributing boxes torn away. Electric leads and cables hung down in festoons, fire-hydrants lay smashed, hoses ripped to shreds, paintwork scorched, blackened and blistered.

Just then Commander Tuck and his party arrived upon the scene and joined the men from the ammunition parties. Tuck decided to open the bulkhead door. Slowly he opened the door and he and Guttridge crawled into the flat wearing long-tubed smoke helmets. Tuck could see fire burning in the hangar above but none in the flat below. Water from the hangar spray system poured through the shattered deck. There seemed to be no serious danger of fire below threatening the magazines – thanks to the prompt action of the hangar spray party – and nothing more could be done.

Bill made his way along to the fore magazines. Here the after magazine crews, their own guns out of action, had joined up to give a hand. Still at it! Good old Gunner's Party!

Tuck came up and said that ammunition was wanted at the guns. With power gone. Bill and his men began to pass the heavy boxes up hand to hand.

Then he went back to the top of the fore magazine. All round the next flat he found rows of badly wounded men on stretchers.

'I'll never be an angel now, sir, I've got to lose me arm,' said one as he passed by. He watched one man being laid gently down. The man carrying him said to the doctor, 'Something went crack as I picked him up, sir.'

'Yes,' said the doctor, 'I'm afraid his back is broken.'

All the time the yammer and thump of the guns, the roar and scream of diving planes, the crump and terrible clangour of bombs, went on above.

During brief lulls everything possible was done to clear the debris away from the guns and keep them firing. At one stage it was reported to Captain Boyd that fire was dangerously near one of the magazines. Would he give permission to flood it? He thought of the *Stukas* and fresh attacks to come. Better the devil you know than the devil you don't, he thought and refused permission.

Down aft Going and his party worked feverishly, putting out fires, opening compartment after compartment looking for dead and wounded. They worked in a terrible and macabre setting. Flames illuminating the water cascading down the lift well made a beautiful and eerie spectacle. Sitting in the reflected glare were the remains of a man with no arms or legs.

By now it looked to Going as it the fires down there were under control, and he ordered everybody out. A warrant officer, Mr Howe, came up and volunteered his help.

'I am not in the habit of giving orders to warrant officers,' said Going, 'but I'm giving you one now. Get to hell out of here!'

He was just about to go himself when there came a terrible shock and roar and he was thrown down. In a great void of blackness he was aware of staggering up and dragging himself up a vertical ladder. Then he passed out.

Another thousand-pound bomb had plunged into the after-lift well. This bomb burst the deck of the lift well and put the steering gear in the compartment below out of action. The ship began to swing crazily round in circles. She remained out of control until Captain Boyd began steering her on main engines alone and headed for Malta.

It was then that her Captain, who loved *Illustrious* so well, went down off the bridge, 'to see,' as he said, 'what they had done to my lovely ship.'

He found *Illustrious* terribly, grievously hurt, her between-decks torn and blackened, with fires still raging, and a very great number of her men dead or seriously injured. He moved among the wounded and badly burned men trying to cheer them with a personal word here and there.

'But,' he said, 'I could not tell one from the other.'

Slowly they fought the ship to Malta, through several more heavy attacks, her stokers maintaining, steam in a temperature of a hundred and forty degrees, with the air vents sucking in thick, acrid smoke, her gunners keeping up a fierce barrage with the fury and blind anger of men who were watching their ship-mates die and agonise all around them, and their beloved, beautiful ship smashed into punch-drunk helplessness.

Bill Banham went aft again, back to the desolation and the stench. Standing by the wrecked keyboard, he saw, undamaged, the Royal Marines' big drum. He passed the American Lieutenant-Commander, who had fought the fires with a damage control party throughout, the battle, and was now going coolly round checking on the damage.

Back on the flight deck Bill met the Captain, looking unperturbed as ever and puffing at his old pipe.

'Poor Mr Anstice,' he said, looking at the blackened, twisted wreck of S2 pom-pom, 'still, never mind, you're still here, you old so-and-so.'

The run-about crane, old Jumbo, looked drunk, hunched black and gaunt, useless. The First Lieutenant was worrying that he had given too much morphia to a badly wounded man. *Never mind. Number One, he'll sleep twice as sound.*

Something was smouldering still at S2 pom-pom. Bill kicked it away... The flight deck was hot to the feet, the after end still obscured by smoke and steam. The stench of burning flesh lay everywhere. At gun quarters great piles of empty brass cordite cylinders sprawled.   '

It was nearly dark now and the list on the ship seemed to be growing worse. Fire still raged in the hangar. Bill was soaked with sea water from the hoses and white with foamite. He was beginning to feel very tired.

More firing? Yes, the pom-poms had started again. It was the last attack of the day. One long, continuous roar of gunfire began again. The firing stopped and they began replenishing empty ready-use lockers once more.

Wearily Bill climbed up through the ladderways and hatchways in the dark on to the flight deck. In the darkness the fires at the after end still glowed. Over on the beam a ship was flashing a message.

The carrier moved slowly forward, uncannily quiet now, except for the hissing of steam.

Somebody broke the silence by saying, 'I can smell the goats in Malta.'

Someone else said, 'Where shall we go tonight, the Vernon or the White Ensign – or Jimmy Bung's bar?'

Everywhere tense nerves quivered in worn-out bodies.

A man suddenly screamed with delayed shock. His oppos took hold of him and quietened him down.

The magazine parties came up, grimy and puffy-eyed, from the stinking darkness that had imprisoned them all day, and asked for news.

The air was brittle. Every noise, every movement now, seemed magnified, an agony. White faces jerked up at every tremor. The ship shuddered as a tug bumped alongside. Word went round that they were entering Grand Harbour.

At last – 'Secure from action stations.'

Everyone came up into the fresh air, clambering stiffly up to the flight deck and gaping dully at the shambles there. As the ship slowly passed the harbour mouth, cheering rose up on either hand. Slowly *Illustrious* came alongside the dockyard wall, then stopped, as it with head bowed.

...What now? A wash? A drink? Ought to. Down to the keyboard flat again. Secondary lights are being rigged. God!

What a mess the place is! The after bulkhead is shut. That's the only way to get down to your cabin. Feel the bulkhead. Seems all right, cold to the touch. Have a fire hose ready, just in case. Open up.

Slowly the door opens. Peer in. Black as hell. An awful stench. Water cascading down in torrents from the hangar deck overhead.

There's the Commander, looking grey and haggard. Great jagged ends of deck plating open downwards from above. Better wait for the lights. Bodies are scattered everywhere. Chaos and utter desolation.

The Warrant Officers' Mess seems all right. Soon small groups of exhausted officers gather there.

You go to the top of the hatchway that leads to your cabin. The iron ladder has been blown away. You're just going to drop down into the darkness below when you see that it is deep in oil and water.

It's nearly midnight now. You've had two days and nights of action stations. You've just gone through all that... You're wet, wretched, and tired enough to flake out where you stand. Your whole body aches. There's the usual crowd in the mess having one. Why not join them? Do you good. Just as you're stepping across the conveyer... 'Oh, I'm piping volunteers to fall in. I want them to go round and collect the dead still lying in the various places. Detail and supervise, will you.'

That drink will have to wait. The men fall in.

'You four, take stretchers into the wardroom. You'll find two officers there, still, one of them lying behind the door. You six go into the ante-room. There's an officer curled round a stanchion there and another underneath him – and one in the corner. You four, go along to that bomb hole. The remains of two of your shipmates are there. Don't leave any pieces about.'

Various parties go round on his ghastly detail, the Gunnery Officer doing the same job in the hangar. Nothing much can be done there. The place is still burning and full of fumes and a fire overhead is shooting down sparks all the time. It's a case of dashing in and getting out quick.

You wander round below through the dark, silent compartments, probing with the torch for more casualties. There are bits of flesh here and there, but only two more bodies.

It's getting light now outside. Dawn. Another day. Have they got all the wounded out of the ship yet? Better go and see, Yes, they've all been taken off in the ambulances.

What's wrong with your legs? You can hardly stand, they are numb from the knees down. The ship, too, seems suddenly to have gone cold.

Must sleep. Have that drink first. Your hand shakes, the glass chatters against your teeth. You gulp it down only to vomit it up again.

You must get warm. Where are you going now? Somewhere for warmth? What about this place, a dynamo room? Yes, it's warm here. You collapse on the deck. The generators hum and vibrate. Suppose action stations sounds again? You'll never hear it down here. Better get up top again.

You wander round in the cold early light, red-eyed and covered with yellow bruises, until the men fall. You mutter a small, all too small, party and drag yourself round, collecting dangerous explosives from every nook and corner in the ship. The day stands still in a haze of stench and filth and unspeakable weariness....

What's that noise? What? What do you say?

Air-raid warning? *Oh God, haven't, they given us enough?*

CHAPTER FOUR

THE LIMEYS

The United States may not have been at war, but no one would have suspected it who saw HMS *Illustrious* met fifty miles off Cape Henry, Virginia, by two US Navy mine-sweepers and escorted down a buoyed and swept channel towards Cape Henry.

The ship had been ordered not to sight land in daylight, and the American sea pilot joined her in the dark off the Cape, flabbergasted that the 'merchantman' he had come out to pick up had turned into a British carrier bearing the scars of war.

There on the blast-swept bridge, over the sad and silent ruin of the pom-poms, the pilot guided her in and round Cape Henry Light. As they rounded the light, suddenly, to the Captain's horror, four searchlights threw their white glare upon the ship, silhouetting her camouflaged shape. So much for security.

From there on it was all light. They steamed past the brilliantly illuminated Virginia Beach and shortly before midnight reached the entrance to the Elizabeth River. At one o'clock, as they approached the fully darkened jetty, the lights were temporarily switched on revealing a reception committee of US Naval officers. Captain MaCandlish, USN, captain of the dockyard, came on board bearing a bottle of whisky and the very touching tribute of a lovely basket of flowers from his wife. The Captain was followed by his technical officers, who were very surprised to find the only means of access a temporary bridge of planks over gaping holes to a curtained-off section of a fire-blackened wardroom.

The American Press was particularly asked for security reasons to keep the British carrier's arrival a secret, and they respected the request handsomely. The US Navy was naturally extremely interested in her, and Mr Secretary Knox immediately paid her a visit as she lay there in Portsmouth Dockyard, USA.

She might have gone to her own Portsmouth Dockyard at home for repairs if the *Luftwaffe* had not already made that impossible. New Fleet Air Arm candidates arriving in Portsmouth one grim January day, about the time *Illustrious* was fighting for her life in the Mediterranean, found themselves in chaos. That night the city had suffered its worst *blitz* and the streets were a shambles. Mud and filfth lay everywhere and a carpet of hoses stopped all traffic on the streets. Everywhere, shops, houses, barracks, still burned, some, their backbones burned right through, collapsing like epileptic giants, others falling swiftly like felled trees as they were dynamited for safety.

It was Norman Hanson's first real sight of the face of war. He had come up from Whitehaven at last, after months of waiting, to face a board for entry into the Fleet Air Arm, and had already, that morning, spent some time waiting in the train in the cold and silent darkness of Hertfordshire, with the engine gently hissing farther up the line, waiting for a reluctant dawn to chase the Dorniers back to the Continent. They were there for a couple of hours, then resumed their journey and Norman caught his connection to Portsmouth.

Portsmouth shocked him, burning and desolate. At Gosport, however, the Navy seemed to be carrying on quite normally.

The Fleet Air Arm candidates were welcomed cheerfully. There were fifty-two of them altogether, fifty-two civilians wondering whether they ought to salute the demi-gods of chief and petty officers who marshalled them with such complete sang-froid.

They knew all about Taranto, of course, these keen young volunteers. They could almost recite the story. What they did not realise was that they themselves had their own Tarantos ahead. This was The Big Adventure for them, the struggle and responsibility which would be their duty did not concern them yet. They knew that *Illustrious* had won Taranto. They did not know that she was, even now, as a result of that very triumph, enduring the same martyrdom that they had seen that day in Portsmouth. They did not know that many of that incomparable few who had gone in over the breakwaters against a fleet, were now dead and that they, civilian rabbits, would have to take their places. All they could think of now was the terrible ordeal of the board which stared them in the face.

The medical was very much simpler than Norman had expected and he passed it with flying colours. But the interview was purgatory....

They sent him out for five minutes of torture in the corridor.

Then he was summoned. He went into the room with his knees knocking. The Admiral cleared his throat and said,

'You want to be a pilot, do you?'

'*Very much*, sir.'

'Right. You're accepted for pilot training – and the best of luck to you.'

'Thank you very much, sir.' He turned to go.

'Oh, and, Hanson....'

'Yes, sir'

'It's probably just as well you didn't want to be an observer. On your mathematics I doubt if they'd let you navigate the Gosport Ferry.'

He was in – no thanks to Euclid.

This was January, 1941, the climax of our finest hour. Although young men were coming forward in their thousands to fill the gaps torn in our strength by Hitler's savage *blitzkrieg*, although planes and ships were coming from factory and yard in an ever-swelling stream, we were still in desperate straits. We were bombed at home, and blitzed by mine, torpedo and Fock-Wulf at sea. In the Mediterranean the *Luftwaffe* had taken over from the ineffectual *Regia Aeronautica* and had begun, with the *Illustrious* blitz, their all-out onslaught on Malta, and the German army, under General Rommel, was building up in North Africa, ready to counter-attack for the Axis and drive us out of the Mediterranean.

They drove *Illustrious* out for a start and sack several fine ships. And they hadn't even begun yet. Behind this first show of strength. Hitler planned a campaign against Greece and Crete for the spring, to coincide with an all-out drive by Rommel in Africa. Between these two giant pincers Wavell's Desert Rats would be crushed in their holes, while the *Luftwaffe* wiped our already battered and depleted Fleet from the sea.

But before he could launch this fury upon us, a greater man than he began a move which was to end with the dictators utter ruin.

On March 11th President Roosevelt's Lend-Lease agreement between Britain and the United States became law. This was good news for the Royal Navy, for it meant that the possibilities of naval supplies and assistance of all kinds immediately increased considerably, and gave the

Naval Division of the British Purchasing Commission in the United States far greater scope.

Illustrious was just in time to come in for one aspect of this increased aid. 'Among other services,' runs the history of the British Delegation to the USA, 'it became possible for British ships to be repaired in US yards, an invaluable asset at a time when British ships were suffering heavy action damage and British yards, particularly in the south of England, were liable to an ever-increasing scale of bombardment from the air.'

And in June another invaluable contribution by Lend-Lease began.

'History of the British Delegation – March 1941 to September 1945... In June 1941, Admiral Towers, USN, the Chief of the Bureau of Aeronautics, informed the British Military Mission that the US Navy had agreed to train some RAF and RN pilots. This offer was immediately accepted by both Admiralty and Air Ministry.'

That was the first step. Shortly afterwards, in July, the United States Secretary of the Navy made a signal which included the authorisation for

'40 RN (Fleet Air Arm) – 1st month; ten in the second month and thirty each succeeding month, for eventual specialised training in carrier type aircraft.'

The new scheme was wonderful news for thirty lucky young sailors at Lee-on-Solent. They had done their basic naval training and now they were to cross the Atlantic to learn to fly, only the second batch of Lend-Lease matelots to do so.

The States! The US Naval Air Corps! Not Luton or Elmdon in blacked-out, wartime Britain, but Pensacola, in Florida, down on the Gulf of Mexico! No more bull and bugles, no more gas and gaiters, no more square-bashing! Gone the fears of failure of 're-scrub', gone the nameless qualms that had assailed them when their names had been called to muster on the cold parade ground.

It didn't matter now – they were going to the States!

They moved on to Manchester,, and Norman and his wife spent two priceless days together. Like most young couples on the eve of separation they talked very little – until it was too late to say all that they wanted to say and her bus was pulling away.

Then, with merciful swiftness, they were moved to Greenock, to board the *Stratheden* for Canada.

After that everything happened with the speed and magic of a movie – Canada, fat with good living, where they spent a fortnight gorging banana splits, *Coca-Cola* and as much chocolate, as much fresh butter and milk, bacon and meat as they could eat, listening to Tommy Dorsey and the US

Navy band, gaping at real Red Indians and holding their breath at a display of high diving by some supermen from MGM. One lovely evening they drove to Niagara and marvelled at the great curtain of atomised white water under floodlights. As for the war – that was a million miles away, unreal. *This was the life!*

They moved on again, and as their train penetrated deeper and deeper into the neutral USA, the rumour of war ebbed even farther away, and became a storm far to sea which did not concern them.

Finally it was journey's end. On a hot, humid afternoon in September their train clanked noisily through the goods yards of Pepsacola on the southern coast of Florida.

The process of learning to fly was hard. First, they sweated at ground school, learning the mysteries of the theory of flight, carburettion and ignition, meteorology and navigation, signalling and trigonometry. Manfully they fought to stay awake while their young American instructors nasally intoned the parable of the adiabatic lapse rate, the Stromberg injection carburettor or the line of thrust.

Then they started flying, and that was much better, though desperately difficult and tiring – take-offs, climbs, glides, turns, Immelmanns, loops, spins and rolls, landings... But there was always Ensign Charlie Culp to see you through, quiet and capable, infinitely patient and friendly, with his eternal:

'Okay, I got her.'

It was a strain, and US Navy standards were very, very tough. But what made all the effort, all the strain bearable, was the superb setting in which all these urgent things were done. Behind it all, cushioning the shocks and setbacks, setting off this ceaseless buzzing of mechanical bees was the lovely, luxuriant backcloth of the Deep South and 'Pensa' itself.

Pensacola was no Nissen City, but a vast Versailles of war laid out immaculately under the Florida sun in stone, brick, concrete and steel, the biggest naval air station in the world.

The British cadets lived in a big, airy block, part of a huge complex of buildings and a place that was a palace of light and comfort after English barracks.

They ate like princes, too. Negro chefs cooked their food – some spicy German, Polish or Italian dish perhaps, or an exotic salad, corn on the cob, melons, cantaloups, ice-cream or 'apple-pie a-la-mode' – and Negro waiters served it to them over immaculate white linen. Milk and butter, ham and eggs, were unlimited.

Ashore, they gorged big T-bone steaks with French fried, potatoes, apple-pie and ice-cream, and usually two or three rum and cokes to wash it all down. On off-duty days they could drink at four in the afternoon or at midnight, if they felt like it.

An automobile hired for the weekend cost the equivalent of a pound a day – a cheap weekend divided among four – and they soon thought nothing of making a round trip of a hundred and ten miles to Mobile, in Alabama, for an evening movie.

> '...So you see,' Norman wrote to Kathleen, 'I can't honestly say I wish I were home with you: rather I wish you were *here* with *me*. There's so much that's new, so much to learAand wonder at.'

Sometimes they were guests of the Florida State College for Women at Tallahassee, the capital of Florida. The Kappa Phi Delta Sorority competed for dances with 'those British boys who talk so cute'.

For recreation – what better than a swim in the wide, blue channel between Santa Rosa Island and the mainland, with the Pratt and Whitneys of the big flying boats thundering out on the deep-water channel? Then, on the station itself, there were tennis and squash courts, baseball pitches, bowling alleys, netball pitches in the magnificent gymnasium, and 'football' fields. You could learn 'Pool', too, that strange game where a beginner can quickly wind up 'behind the eight ball'.

Highlight of the station's facilities for entertainment was a great auditorium. In the daytime it was a comfortable and acoustically perfect lecture-hall, in the off-duty hours it became a magnificent theatre, with a movie show every evening and a change of programme nightly.

Somebody found out that Norman played the piano and organ, and he was roped in as resident organist, in conjunction with Eddie Osborne, a US instructor and former cinema organist. He went very willingly, as the organ was a magnificent one. On weekday evenings he played swing, with the exception of the regular Friday night concert and sing-song, when he played popular classics, with the Warsaw Concerto top of the Pensacola hit parade.

Often they were invited to the gracious homes of well-to-do Southerners, most of whom seemed to have a morbid interest in the bombing of London. The British cadets would chat politely, sipping tall mint juleps with what they hoped was that 'typical British reserve'. At one of these gatherings, Norman noted, Jim Flockhart, whose naval service is about three months longer than mine, told a spell-bound audience how he sat in a submarine with Lord Louis Mountbatten at the bottom of Hamburg harbour, playing bridge until the depth-charging left off!

Sunday mornings at Pensacola were always especially pleasant. They could take a rest from the strain of learning to fly – lie in bed until nine, take a leisurely shower, shave, dress and drift over the Ship's Service for a snack and a cup of coffee.

Sunday, December 7th, 1941, was just such a morning. The weather was spring-like, sunny and warm. In Hanson's dormitory they were idly dressing, reading, writing letters home or just loafing. From all the dormitories along their floor, radios churned out the transmissions of the Pensacola district network. Swing records were interrupted regularly by exhortations to 'buy that bedroom suite at Weitzelmann's – A new *low* in price and an all-time high in quality!' or by a close harmony quartet who urged:

> *Let's all so to Sorority Shop,*
> *Sorority Shop, Sorority Shop!*
> *Let's all go to Sorority Shop*
> *For the clothes that you'll adore!*

A deep, masculine voice followed this one with advice to young ladies about to get married:

'Buy your wedding gown at Sorority! You owe it – to HIM!'

The commercials bubbled on.

Then came an interruption that was not about wardrobes or trousseaux at all. A voice had just been singing:

> *'I doan wanna set the world on fi-yer...'*

When it was cut out for an announcer to say breathlessly that at that very moment Japanese planes were bombing the US Naval Base at Pearl Harbour.

He went off the air and the crooner came back...

> *'...doan wanna set the world on fi-yer,*
> *I just wanna start a flame in your heart...'*

'*Flash!*' came the announcers voice again. 'First reports indicate...'

And so it was told to an incredulous America, that bloody tale of disaster and double-dealing. Japanese aircraft operating from an unknown base were making a hell of Hawaii.

About three in the afternoon Norman Hanson joined his instructor, Charlie Culp, in the bar of the *San Carlos Hotel*. This time they drank as allies, joining together in the most obscene abuse of Japanese and Germans alike that they could muster, before they drowned it all in rye.

So the United States came into the war and Old Glory shook out its folds to the storm. Overnight a fever for war spread over the country, a fire of hate for the Japanese.

On the station now it was 'bud' all the time. The Limeys were OK now, four zee-ro, yes sir! No longer were they 'the guys who ran from Dunkirk'.

The British were accosted every other minute. Girls. Everywhere they went – girls, most of them easy on the eye,, too, young, dark, appealing, catching the eye in restaurants, in bars, in night-clubs, even in shops..

Perhaps it was just as well that tfaey were plunged back into flying....

It *was* like a plunge – into a sobering bath of icy water. For it was winter now and cold as charity when they 'bussed out' to the field at seven-thirty in the morning, frozen and half-asleep inside their greatcoats. Out in the yellow trainers they practised blind flying in a covered cockpit, trying to home on service radio ranges, to recover from unusual positions and to execute long climbing turns and sweeping glides.

It was tough and they were all very tired by now. But you couldn't fail now, for this was almost the last lap. Now the way divided – wings or no wings. Failure was unthinkable.

One night a very weary Acting Leading Naval Airman Hanson turned in for an uneasy sleep. The cadets' course was finished.

Had he passed?

The next night he got no sleep at all, for he was Temporary Acting Sub-Lieutenant (A) N S Hanson, RNVR, and would wear bell-bottoms no longer. As he put up the single wavy gold band, surmounted by those longed-for wings, he felt that life could hold no greater moment.

The new pilots moved on for the last stage in their training to Miami. Their streamliner flashed on rails of silver down the coast through Daytona, West Palm Beach and Fort Lauderdale, then slowed and braked quietly to a standstill in Miami station.

Immediately hundreds of holiday-makers swarmed out into the Florida sunshine.

'You guys for the station? Okay, there's the bus. Get in.'

And off they went, a slightly swollen-headed bunch of young – flying sailors. The US Naval Air Station at Miami produced all the fighters pilots for the Fleet, and the Britishers were all going to be 'single seat men'. The prospect was thrilling and accounted for much of that high-octane feeling in the head. The rest could be blamed on the disturbing effect of fabulous Miami, the luxury never-never land, remote as Hollywood.

'Okay, I got her. Say, feller, you just *cain't* get away with that side-slippin' in. There ain't nothin' takes off an undercart faster, boy.'

He was back on dual instruction.

'Next thing you know we're in the sonofabitch of a cra-a-ash and bustin' our asses!'

Lieutenant Klinsman, USN, was doing the talking. Norman was trying powered landings for the first time.

'Okay, let's go in again. Now give her some right rudder as you pour that gas in.'

The Harvards certainly called for dual control at this stage. They were hot-tempered animals after the gentle biplanes at Pensa. They had considerably reduced lift and a number of complicated 'mod cons' such as constant-speed propellers, retractable undercarriages, landing flaps and steerable tail wheels.

Eventually Klinsman let him solo with:

'I guess yuh oughta live. I cain't see more'n fifty reasons why you shouldn't.'

Then he flew a fighter for the first time.

Outside on the tarmac in the crisp, clear morning sunshine stood the tubby little Brewster Buffaloes, like big, metallic bumble-bees. The props flung shimmering vortices of rainbow vapour. There was a great, hot roar from open exhausts. Then mechanics cut the engines, the roar died, exhausts popped and were silent.

The windsocks are rigid. Okay, out you go!

There's your Buffalo, squat, barrel-shaped, lethal – twelve hundred horsepower under its bulky cowling. A mechanic on the wing grabs the chute and drops it into the bucket seat. You toss the harness straps open, the buckles clang on metal. A jump, a snatch at the windscreen, and you're in the cockpit. The mechanic passes the chute straps over your shoulders and clips them into position on your chest. You pass the other two round your thighs and secure them. Then you fasten the safety harness and tighten it up.

'Okay?'

'Yes, okay.'

On booster pump. Prime the engine... that's enough. Throttle setting? Mixture setting? Okay. Magnetos switched on. All ready.

'Stand clear!' from the mechanic.

Thumbs up. Press tfae starter switch.

A couple of husky coughs, a muffled chugging, end she starts first shot. Mixture control hard over to 'rich', throttle back a little. Set it to idle at 1,100 revs per minute.

Look round the office and check for take-off. (You've done all this a thousand times in theory, swotted every lever, every -switch.) Flaps – up. Petrol cock – main tank. Pitch control – maximum revs. Mixture – full rich. Hydraulic pressure – OK. Oil pressure – almost OK. Temperature – still on the low side, but she'll warm up before I get off. Radio connected and switched on. Tail wheel unlocked.

Ready to go.

Oil pressure normal now. Temperature OK. Open the throttle till the RPM counter shows two thousand revs. Switch from 'Both' to 'R – 30 drop'. Back to 'Both'. Now to 'L – 50 drop'. Well within safety limits.

Throttle back and wag the left hand – chokes away. The plane captain beckons directing you to the perimeter track. You zig-zag slowly round to the duty runway. The Duty Officer waves 'Come on!' A touch of left brake and a short burst of throttle brings you on the runway. Tail wheel locked, goggles down, harness locked.

Open the throttle slowly. Quicker now – to full.

A surge of engine hurls the machine forward, pushing you back against the head-rest. With tail well up you scream-down the runway. Juggle the rudder to keep her straight. Then with a delicate pull on the stick... you're airborne!

The ground slips quickly away as you climb, fast and straight. Wheels up – the indicators slowly climb to 'Locker Up'. Throttle back to climbing boost, pull the pitch control out to climbing revs, close the hood.

The engine thunders away, never tiring. There are new noises now, and disconcerting vibrations to get used to. But this is power – at last!

It's me, Norman Hanson from Whitehaven, flying a fighter in the Florida skies – a single-seat man!

The sun shines warm through the 'greenhouse'. As you lift your goggles you feel sweat on the bridge of your nose. Down there is Miami Beach, the white villas glistening in the sun. *Yesterday evening I was down there, amidst the music and bright lights, soaking it up at Winnie's bar.*

After this there still remained a lot of hard training on the Buffalo. They did a lot of night flying, which was sheer pleasure. The coastline was well illuminated, there was always a 'Miami moon' and the airfield, on their return, was like Piccadilly Circus – just 'follow the red light' for a safe landing. On these occasions there was even an instructor at the end of the runway talking to them on the R/T.

'You're too high, son, and get that manifold pressure down a coupla jerks. *Now* you got it! Hold it there, feller, you're dead in the groove!'

Those night solos in a fast machine, alone above the earth in a blackness lit by stars far above them and the warm lights of home and glittering hotels remote below, had a pure and lovely enchantment all their own. Miami, and fighters, were a sort of coming-of-age.

And in their coming-out *Illustrious* had a hand. For at Miami they were closely supervised by the Chief Instructor for RN Fighter Training in the

USA – Lieutenant-Commander C L G Evans, DSC, RN.

He still had that fierce red beard. Now he earned a stick and sported a knitted silk tie. He was the Americans' idea of the perfect 'Limey'.

As such he made their opinion of his kind go up by leaps and bounds, as high as his already fabulous achievements in the air. He outflew every US Navy instructor on the station with non-chalant and infuriating ease, and, above all, made sure that his charges were taught from the book of battle experience. Any US critic of the Royal Navy's way of doing things was liable to be greeted with a tilt of those wicked eyebrows and a polite but definite hint that he had better 'get some time in' before he presumed to pass judgement on tactics that had been learned the hard way – against the *Luftwaffe* on Malta convoy and in the Atlantic.

Then came the final check-out. After that the fully-blown fighter pilot could put in his log book:

> 'Completed RN Fighter Training: 9.4.42.
> Ability as Pupil Fighter Pilot: AVERAGE.'

Average. 'Oh, well,' thought Norman, 'it could have been worse.' He could have been dead, like the lad who had spun his Buffalo in only the day before. 'Anyway, it'll probably see me through,' he wrote.

Two days later Uncle Sam shook his hand and gave him his formal blessing, as the Captain of Miami handed him the diploma which read:

> 'Know all men by these presents that Sub-Lieutenant Norman S Hanson, RNVR, has met successfully the requirements of the course as prescribed for Naval Aviators of the United States Navy.'

'It was quite a moment,' he told Kathleen in person, just three weeks later.

CHAPTER FIVE

No Uncertain Sound

Glorious and *Courageous* of the Navy's Old Contemptibles had long since gone. *Ark Royal* had been sunk on November 14th, 1941, off Sardinia; *Hermes* was sent to the bottom in April 1942 by Japanese carrier planes in the Indian Ocean,

In May of 1942, however, *Illustrious* and *Indomitable*, the two sisters built side by side at Barrow, co-operated, under *Illustrious'* old skipper, Denis Boyd, in the combined operation against Madagascar, in which for the first time a carrier-borne striking force of the Royal Navy was used to provide fighter cover for troops ashore, until airfields could be secured. This operation was the opening gambit in the new expansion of Allied activities into the great, worldwide offensive tfaat would run Germans and Japanese off their feet to final collapse. It was the first victory for Britain after three years of desperate defensive, the beginning of a new order and the end of an old.

There was a setback in August, when the epic convoy to Malta passed through from west to east in that month. *Eagle*, as well as the cruisers *Cairo* and *Manchester*, was torpedoed and sunk, and *Indomitable* badly damaged by bombs. Of the carriers present, only the *Victorious*, whose aircraft had earlier helped to find and sink the *Bismarck*, and the old *Furious* came off unscathed, and eleven of the fourteen merchant ships were lost, but *Furious* flew off a further reinforcement of Spitfires to Malta, and the three merchantmen which did get in kept the island in rations for another four months.

In May and June of the same year, the battles of Coral Sea and Midway saw the Japanese Fleet routed by the carriers of the US Fleet, and in August the US Marines, at heavy cost, got a foothold on Guadalcanal and held it as the new advanced base for the attack on Japan's outer bastion of islands. In September, Rommel, his supply line slashed by Allied aircraft and submarines, was beaten at Alam Halfa, and on October 23rd the Eighth Army, built up to great strength via the Cape and Suez, attacked him at El Alamein. By November 3rd he had been badly beaten and was falling back.

Then, on November 8th, the Allied armies landed in North Africa. Fleet Air Arm Seafires and Wildcats helped to give them air cover; *Victorious* and *Formidable* were there, with furious to represent the Old Guard and a number of the new escort carriers pointing to an important new development.

The year 1943 came in with the strength of British naval aviation growing all the time. The Navy was concentrating on fighters now. Naval bomber strength had always been ahead and looked in a fairly healthy state now, with the new British-built Barracuda coming into service and the American Avenger promised for the future. But the Navy had never had enough fighters. With the RAF enjoying almost exclusive priority in new fighter production for the first three years of the war, the Fleet Air Arm had had to do the vital job of protectmg the fleet and the convoys at sea with a few obsolete Sea Gladiators and the slow Fulmars. Our war effort – and our sailors – had suffered accordingly. Then, grudgingly, they were given some Hurricane I's, still outclassed and outnumbered. Now, after a stiff fight, they had the Seafire and, biggest blessing of all, for the Seafire was only a short-range fighter, naval aircraft especially designed and built for the job were reaching them from American factories.

In July, *Formidable* and *Indomitable* supported the invasion of Sicily, and in September, when Allied troops were landed at Salerno on the Italian mainland, the Fleet Air Arm was there in force. Five escort carriers under Rear-Admiral Vian gave air cover over the beaches, while *Illustrious* and *Formidable* protected the small carriers themselves.

Norman Hanson, a lieutenant now, was posted to St Merryn at the end of April.

'Seafires!' he wrote jubilantly in his diary. '*Now* we'll show 'em a thing or two!'

But it was not to be. To his intense disappointment, with only, one hour and forty minutes of Seafire time in his log, he was told that the machines booked for his new squadron had been switched elsewhere. With nothing to do, they were sent off on a week's compulsory leave. Norman travelled for nineteen uncomfortable hours to Carlisle, where his wife was living with her mother, and, after a couple of days with Kathleen, started off on the return journey to Cornwall. When he had got as far as Exeter he met one of the instructors from St Merryn.

'Hello,' said the instructor. 'You're Hanson, aren't you?'

'That's right,' said Norman warily.

'Aren't you supposed to be in America?'

'Not me,' said Norman. 'I've been there.'

'Well, I don't know, I may be wrong, but I thought I saw your name up for a draft to the States.'

When Norman got to St Merryn that night, tired and fed up, he was told to report to the CO at nine o'clock the next morning.

He did so. It was right – the States again. He was to report right away to Donibristle, in Scotland, to join the nucleus of 1833 Squadron, which was forming there. With weary resignation he got on the train once more and did the nineteen hours back to Carlisle, *en route* for Donibristle. Perhaps *this* time he might really be joining an operational squadron.

It was the real thing all right, the appointment he had been waiting for ever since that passing-out day at Miami Fighter School.

There were four of them at Donibristle altogether, the most experienced pilots of the new squadron. Hanson was to be Senior Pilot, under the squadron's commanding officer, Lieutenant-Commander H A Monk, DSM and Bar, RN. With them were two RNVR Sub-Lieutenants, Starkey and Boddington.

The CO was a hard case. He was RN, and did not altogether approve of such ninety-day wonders as RNVR pilots. He had joined the Royal Navy at the age of fifteen as a boy seaman and had fought his way, by drive and intelligence, up to the rank of Lieutenant-Commander. He was already a Fleet Air Arm ace. His Distinguished Service Medal and Bar he had won in Norwegian waters aboard *Ark Royal*. In person short, strong and vital, he was a fine, aggressive pilot, a real 'fighter'. He did not believe in coddling the ex-civilians just because they had only been in the Service a dog-watch. Monk had seen far too much war for that He was now twenty-five, years old, three years younger than his Senior Pilot.

These four men were the core of the as yet shadowy unit known as 1833 Squadron Royal Navy. The squadron was to equip with new American fighter aircraft, which they would pick up in the United States. The CO, Hanson, Starkey and Boddington were to be joined by the other pilots – all newly-trained single-seat men from Miami Fighter School – when they reached Yankeeland.

The four pilots, together with the squadron ratings, went by train to Liverpool, on their way to Norfolk, Virginia. They took passages, unescorted, in the fast liner *Empress of Scotland*, in company with a big naval draft for ships fitting out in American yards and eleven hundred *Afrika Korps* prisoners.

From Norfolk they piled aboard a special train for New York. Here they split up, the ratings going to the US Navy barracks at Asbury Park, and the officers to the 'RN Hotel', otherwise the *Brabizon Plaza*, 57th Street West. They loafed here, in luxurious accommodation, not a heaving-line's distance from the fleshpots of wartime New York, for fourteen days.

It was during these fourteen days tfaat the rumours started.

By now they knew two things about thheir future. First – they were to go to the US Navy fighter airfield at Quonset Point, Rhode Island. Second – they were to fly Corsairs, only the third British squadron to be equipped with these machines, following 1830 and 1831. Quonset was conveniently near the Chance-Vought works at Stratford, Connecticut.

One or two of them had already heard the buzz about the Chance-Vought Corsair F4U. Now they began to hear more and more of its fearsome reputation. Daily, stories came in of casualties among American trainees at Quonset Point – all on Corsairs. The fearful brute, it seemed, was killing off American pilots quicker than the Japs could do it. There were blood-curdling rumours of spinning-in and other forms of sudden death. After all, there must be something in the buzz – hadn't the US Navy temporarily discarded Corsairs as being too dangerous for carrier work and given them to their own Marine Corps and the British? The Fleet Air Arm had never yet been given something for nothing.

So the new squadron waited uneasily for the move to Rhode Island. By now they had all assembled. The new pilots had joined, some straight from Miami, and some from stooge jobs which had kept them occupied before the whole squadron could meet.

The new boys came from all parts of tfae Empire. Sub-Lieutenant J R ('Johnny') Baker, Royal Canadian Naval Volunteer Reserve, came from Toronto. He was a big, husky Canuck, with a younger brother in tbe Fleet Air Arm. His father, Colonel Baker, had founded the Canadian Institute for the Blind, having himself been blinded by gas in the Great War. Gordon Aitken was an ex-public schoolboy who had been born in Ceylon, where his father, a planter, still lived. Gordon was destined to meet his father rather sooner than he bad expected. Eric Rogers, very young and very noisy, came from 'Brum'. Peter Builder was also very young. Neil Brynildsen was one of the many New Zealanders to serve with the Fleet Air Arm. Finally, there was W K ('Bash') Munnoch, from Middlesbrough, an ex-Marine.

This was 1833 Fighter Squadron of the Royal Navy. With the CO, Norman Hanson, Starkey and Boddington, there were ten of them – so far. Ahead of them was the Corsair.

One warm summer afternoon they arrived at Quonset. With to accustomed thoroughtness the US Navy had made complete preparations for them.

They were told that their machines awaited them over in the hangar which they had been allotted. When Monk and Hanson and Air Artificer 'Wolf' Madison, their chief maintenance man, went over to the hangar they got a surprise.

The building was in darkness. They made their way up the steps leading to the balcony round the top deck of the hangar and started exploring the rooms there. To their amazement they discovered that their reception had been laid on down to the last meticulous detail. Well-equipped offices had been allotted to the squadron and there was even a desk for the Senior Pilot and one, too, for 'Chiefie' Madison. Everything was there, down to the sharply pointed pencils on the blotters.

'We're going to win the war,' said Normm.

The vast hangar below was still in darkness.

'Well, we'd better have a look at them,' said the CO. Seeing a rating down below, he shouted to him to put the hangar lights on.

'Okay, bud,' came the answer.

Monk's blood pressure rose visibly, but he contained himself.

The lights went on like an explosion and it was then that they saw their aircraft for the first time.

They stood and stared. Then Norman Hanson broke off and went into tthe nearest office. The sound of typing was heard.

'What the hell are you doing?' said Monk.

'Let's talk of wills and name executors,' said Norman. 'At least, that's what *I'm* doing!'

He had just had his first look at 'the bent-wing bastard from Stratford'.

The Corsairs were lined up down each side of the hangar, silent, hunched, like savage beasts asleep or waiting to pounce.

General impressions were frightening enough. A closer inspection gave them real grounds for their fears.

Norman found himself gawping at a big, heavy aeroplane, larger than any fighter he had ever seen before. An enormously long nose ended bluntly for'd in the big radial engine cowling, the light glinting on the blue-black oily sheen of the bulging Pratt and Whitney engine inside. Up in front, behind a long, sausage-shaped spinner, was a gigantic three-bladed airscrew, one tapering steel blade almost touching the ground. Somewhere about half a mile back from the nose was sunk a cockpit. It didn't look as if you would be able to see anything but nose from there. Behind the cockpit the fuselage knifed back gracefully and briefly to a big tailplane, fin and rudder. Most strange and astonishing of all, however, was the Corsair's great wing. From the wing root, thick as a wrestlers thigh, the wing swept sharply down, then up again, to the wing tip. It was a big, metal, inverted Seagull's wing, with the fuselage perched high in the middle – appropriate enough for a naval fighter but flamboyant and fearsome to the eyes of those gently bred to the demure Fulmar and the sleek, classic Seafire.

And tomorrow tfaey were to go in the cage with these brutes – alone! Norman was not the only one who made his will that day.

But they did not tackle the Corsairs right away. First came lectures and the intensive study of handling notes. Then, and only then, did they climb into the cockpit.

> 'Then began for everyone,' says the Squadron Line Book, 'a period of intensive study, until what at first had appeared to be the nightmare of a bloke what plays a one man band resolved itself into a reasonably comfortable office.'

In the midst of the handling notes they found a sinister warning:

> Aircraft will not, repeat NOT recover from a spin.

This was not amusing. Norman remembered with warmth and affection the days of controlled – spins at Pensacola. Now, it seemed, if you spun in *any* attitude, you died. The early versions of the Corsair, so went the scuttlebutt, had actually been fitted with spin chutes which could be operated by a lever in the cockpit and helped to recover from the death dive.

There could be no doubt, of course, that the Corsair was a fine piece of engineering. The inverted gull wing, a brilliant innovation, raised the fuselage so that the powerful Pratt and Whitney engine had room to swing the big thirteen-foot propeller, and reduced drag considerably by its ninety-degree interception with the fuselage and its backward retracting undercarriage – a short, sturdy affair with the robustness necessary for carrier landings. Also incorporated in the big, six-ton fighter was a hydraulic system by which the pilot could fold the wings, open and shut engine cowlings and air cooler ventilators, operate the undercarriage and deck-hook, and by which the six .5-inch machine-guns could be loaded.

It was a novel machine, a fast (four-hundred-knot), powerful fighting brute, and there were still some 'bugs' to be got rid of in its design. The pilot's view, for example, was bad. The designers, in order to give the Corsair its great operational range, had added big, self-sealing fuel tanks to the prototype fuselage and unfortunately they had had to move the cockpit three feet farther aft to make room for them. This handicapped the pilots field of vision, which was limited anyway by the long nose. To cure this the cockpit was raised in later models and a bigger 'bubble' canopy fitted.

But 1833 Squadron's Corsairs still had the old cockpits, and the pilots found the view a bit too restricted for comfort. And they were definitely not built for short men. Norman was lucky, being tall and wiry, but if you were on the short side you could see very little from the cockpit. If, on the other hand, you had your seat raised to improve your view, your feet would not reach the rudder pedals. Corsairs, obviously, had been built for those big, husky American boys!

They started learning the Corsair by the approved US Navy method of going straight into aerobatics to find out just how the brute behaved, fanatically carefully of course not to do anything to make it spin.

They had a few prangs. Neil Brynildsen, the New Zealander, put his machine up on its nose on the third day of training, fracturing the airscrew rather neatly, and a little later 'Steve' Starkey braked too hard when swerving off the runway and went right over on his back. However, nobody was hurt in these minor mishaps and for the first eight days training went reasonably smoothly.

Then, on the ninth day, came tragedy. Boddington, coming into Quonset from seaward over the inlet, stalled in the slip-stream of an Avenger which was coming in just ahead of him and went straight into the sea. An American sailor out with his girl happened to see the Corsair crash and was able to pinpoint the spot.

Boddington was still in the cockpit when they found the wreckage. There was a wound on his head which would have knocked him out but not killed him. As he was still strapped in, he must have drowned while still unconscious.

The machine itself was a broken chaos. It was brought up in two pieces. The engine had been wrenched off with the shock and the airscrew blades were wrapped round the shattered cowling like lettuce leaves.

The CO and Johnny Baker, the duty pilot, went over to Newport to identify the body. His death was a terrible shock for his parents.

Photographs of the funeral service were sent to his father, who was Mayor of Croydon that year.

It was a very chastened, saddened group of men who started their tenth day of training.

But there were no more fatalities. Reggie Shaw, very young, very quiet and very much a Londoner; came into the squadron in place of Boddington and they went steadily on through their six weeks' working up at Quonset hard on the heels of 1830 and 1831 squadrons, with the CO driving them harder and harder all the time. Then they were moved to fresh fields and pastures new.

Their space at Quonset was needed for the US Marines, who were getting more and more of the U-birds from Stratford. This was partly because they were having such success with them, operating from island airstrips in the Pacific, and partly because the carrier pilots of the US Navy were not.

For the biggest snag of all at this stage in the Corsair story was the F4U's black record as a deck lander. The sad tale was that the otherwise excellent landing gear of the machine had a built-in bounce. The compression of air and oil inside the eleopneumatic struts when the Corsair made a heavy carrier touch-down promptly reacted and bounced the big aircraft up again and clear over the arrester wires.

This was the story 1833 had heard. This was the main reason why the US Marine Corps were using Corsairs in increasing numbers from their airstrips in the Solomons, and why the Royal Navy, which had to come cap in hand for aircraft to America, was getting the prancing F4U instead of the Grumnian Hellcat, which the carriers of the US Navy were now adopting exclusively.

The rate of accidents in deck landing Corsairs mounted so viciously throughout 1943 that the machine was very nearly declared unfit for sea duty. However, the Chance-Vought engineers went feverishly to work and managed to cure the undercarriage and remove the bounce.

But the modification was not to reach 1833 until they were a long way from Rhode Island. In the meantime they had a lot of deck landing to do. Very soon they would have to fly their Corsairs aboard a training carrier in American waters. What would happen then was anybody's guess.

Meanwhile they moved from Quonset Point to a new airfield at Brunswick, Maine. They had had a wild binge the night before and they went off the runway in all attitudes next morning – all except the CO, who did not drink and took the poorest view of RNVR's who did.

Norman, more dead than alive, opened up his Corsair and hopped off down the runway. Jumping and stalling, jumping and stalling, past caring what happened, and did the three hundred miles to Brunswick like a zombie.

At Brunswick 1833 began on intensified version of the kind of training they had been doing at Quonset. They practised open escort line-abreast formation, breaking up to right and left when the attacking force of friendly fighters jumped them. For air-to-air firing practice one of their own Corsairs acted as drogue tower. There was plenty of air-to-ground firing too, with the F4U's carrying out furious ramrods upon rocks out at sea. They bounced their way through Aerodrome Dummy Deck Landings on a piece of airfield marked out like a carrier's deck, and hoped they would be able to do the same on real carriers without breaking their necks. These 'ADDL's' were done over at Rockland, in Maine, with Norman Hanson and the CO acting as deck-landing control officers, each taking the bats in turn and bringing the rest in, while the other made his pass at the 'deck'.

Maine was beautiful in autumn and rather like Norway, Norman thought. They flew over forests, deep green, red-gold and russet, and over inlets shimmering in the gentle sunshine. It was hard to imagine a more gently beautiful scene, hard to tell himself that this small, noisy world of roaring'engines and hammering guns was his reality, and not the peaceful forests, warm with the earth's welcome, calm with freedom from fear.

They put in many hours of low-flying practice over the sea, and the irrepressible young Eric Rogers went down so low that he put his propeller in the sea and, with beginner's luck, actually got away with it. The first the others knew about it was when Eric's Corsair started to give a striking impersonation of an egg whisk and showered his wingman with spray.

So far nobody had got into a spin. But it had to happen sometime and one day it happened to Norman.

He was practising dog-fighting tactics with Starkey. The two Corsairs were approaching each other on reciprocal courses, with Starkey two thousand feet above Norman. The idea was for the man with the height advantage to break off as soon as he came above the other and try to get on his tail. This time Starkey cheated, cut a corner and, when Norman looked round, was just getting himself into a cosy firing position. Norman, surprised, whipped round quickly and a bit hamfistedly and – went into a spin.

The result was terrifying. A frightful clangour, a great hammering on all the tail surfaces, an unearthly clatter of hysterical air on metal, accompanied a frantic, palsied shaking and shuddering of the whole aircraft.

He tried to recover, putting on opposite rudder to the direction of the spin. Nothing happened. Again and again he hit right rudder hard, but the aircraft would not come out – still the insane, frightening yammering and shaking with the Corsair screammg round in a corkscrew to port.

Aircraft will not, repeat NOT recover from a spin.

Yes... time to bale out. He started to loosen his harness.

He looked at his height. Nine thousand feet. I'll have one more shot, he thought, then I'll get to hell out of here.

The plane was not really in a complete spin – there had not been enough left rudder on in the first place. So he put all his eggs in one basket and hit left rudder hard to finish the job properly.

He was spinning now all right. Would the Corsair recover?

Theory said no.

Here goes.

He slammed on right rudder as hard as he could.

The Corsair did another one and a half turns, then steadied.

He put the stick forward and she came out.

They were going very fast and diving steeply. But they were out. So he shut the hood again and went home. He was never quite as afraid of Corsairs again.

They were all feeling the strain a bit now. The Corsairs were enough to give anyone nerves, and with the CO driving them hard, day in, day out, to bring them to the standard he knew was vital for battle, some of the younger ones began to 'twitch'.

And now the squadron was due to go to Norfolk, Virginia, and follow the Corsairs of 1830 and 1831 by doing deck-landing training aboard the escort carrier *Charger*.

Norman's log-book recorded the next move.

'Oct 14. Brunswick to Floyd Bennett Field, New York.

'Oct. 15. Floyd Bennett and return. (Unsuccessful attempt to reach Norfolk: bad weather.)'

It was frustrating, but it did postpone the evil day.

'Oct. 17. Floyd Bennett Field to Norfolk.'

But at Norfolk there, was a stoppage on the production line. The deck landings were cancelled and they never saw the *Charger*. With mixed feelings of relief and anti-climax 1833 prepared for home.

On a black, rainy morning in October they arrived aboard the escort carrier *Trumpeter* in Belfast Lough, after a comparatively uneventful crossing from Norfolk. They had come over in a fast convoy at a time when the Allies were beginnng to get a grip on the U-boats. The escorts had been busy with their depth-charges, but no real attacks had developed and no ships had been lost.

Trumpeter nosed alongside a jetty abutting Sydennam Airfield, to the east of Belfast, where cranes swiftly off-loaded the Corsairs of 1830, 1831 and 1833, the first Royal Navy squadrons to bring the new machines to Britain for use with the Fleet.

At Sydenham it rained solidly for three days and nights and they waited miserably for it to clear. Eventually the CO had had enough. Glaring fiercely at a gleam of light which was blinking timidly through the overcast, he announced, 'We're going, Hans: get them organised!'

In fifteen minutes' time the pilots, complete with pyjamas and toothbrush, bundled into their Corsairs. Soon the engines were snarling and propellers sucking up miniature waterspouts from the rain-soaked tarmac.

The CO taxied out at a cracking pace, zig-zagging off down the perimeter, with Gordon Aitken and Eric Rogers behind him.

The rest followed. The runway was a shade narrow but they got away in pairs and soon formed up in three vicks of three over the field. Then they set course for Stretton, near Warrington, in Lancashire.

They climbed to clear the hills, slid-through the band of silver light, and emerged into the sunshine over the Irish Sea. Below them they caught sight of the Isle of Man, lying like a grey cloud on the sea. They roared on and glided down into Liverpool Bay.

The sky was still bright and clear around them, but Lancashire looked foreboding, with a veil of black cloud across its face.

Before they had time to worry:

'Hello, Charlie Orange! My engine's packing in. Christ! Look at this lot....'

They looked. Eric's engine was coughing out great gouts of black smoke.

There's a merchant ship down there to port. Go down and ditch by him,' ordered Monk.

'Like hell! Not with all the loot I've got aboard!' flashed Eric.

'All right then. Hans, detach one of your chaps to look after him.'

'Okay, boss. Number four, you stay with him and see what happens to him.'

'Wilco, Hans.' Reggie Shaw's Corsair broke away and joined the lame duck.

The rest of them headed on through the muck, heading for their landing ground at Stretton.

In the middle of the filthy black cloud, Steve Starkey lost the others. Luckily, however, Steve was a native of Ellesmere Port, nearby. As soon as he found himself alone he immediately hit low level for home, found it, and from there hedge-hopped down the familiar highways and byways to

New aircraft carrier launched. HMS Illustrious, *the largest aircraft carrier yet built for the Royal Navy, was launched from the yard of Messrs. Vickers-Armstrong, Ltd., at Barrow in Furness on 5th April, 1939. The naming ceremony was performed by Lady Henderson, wife of Admiral Sir Reginald Henderson.*

Another picture of the No. 732, HMS Illustrious *in the Walney Channel, tugs seizing her and towed her along to the fitting-out basin in Buccleugh Dock.*

Fighter plane aboard HMS Illustrious.

The Ordeal of HMS Illustrious. German dive-bombers begin their attack at 12.35 pm on 10th January, 1941. The Illustrious is with the Fleet, a hundred miles west of Malta.

The aircraft carrier HMS Illustrious is almost hidden by spray and smoke from bomb bursts during a savage German dive-bombing attack in the Mediterranean.

Italian Barrage Balloon of the same design that were placed around Tarranto.

Admiral Sir Lumbey St G Lyster, KCB, CVO, DSO (right)

Swordfish in close formation flying back from another sortie.

HMS Illustrious, *re-commissioned after a refitting in American and British dockyards, seen from the cockpit of an American built Martlet fighter plane based on the* Illustrious. *The ship suffered extensive damage during dive-bombing attacks in the Mediterranean.*

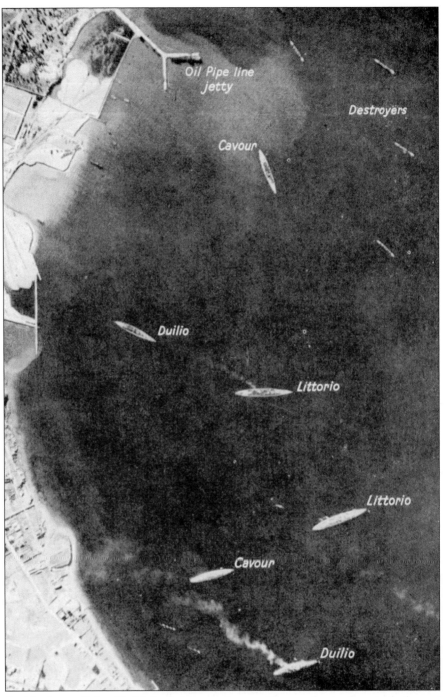

Oil Pipe line
jetty

Destroyers

Cavour

Duilio

Littorio

Littorio

Cavour

Duilio

In this picture all six of Italy's battleships are shown safely at anchor in the outer harbour at Taranto. This was taken on the 10th November. Next day the Fleet Air Arm from Illustrious *attacked and disabled half of them with torpedos and bombs.*

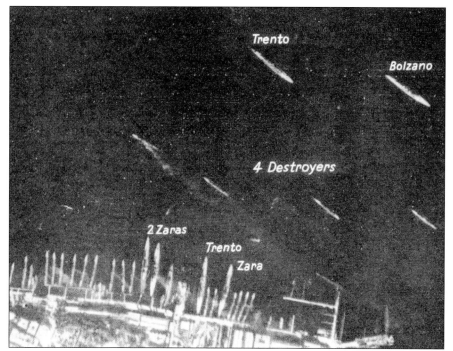

This picture shows the inner harbour at Tarranto the day before the Fleet Air Arm attack. After The two cruisers, of the Bolzano and Trento classes, have heeled over and were heavily damaged.

24-29 January 1945 – Fleet Air Arm strikes on oil installations at Pladjoe around Palembang, Sumatra – the largest operation ever undertaken by the Fleet Air Arm – successful strikes are made by aircraft from Task Force 63 – HM carriers Indomitable, Illustrious, Indefatigable *and* Victorious.

US naval aircraft flew not only from American decks: as the naval threat in Europe eased, the Royal Navy assigned carriers to the war in the Pacific, carriers whose air groups were largely composed of American aircraft. Typical was this Avenger II (TBM-1C) ready on the catapult on HMS Illustrious, *17 December, 1944.*

Admiral James Somerville sampling the Ice Cream on USS Saratoga, *1944.*

Admiral Moody, as Admiral Commanding Aircraft Carriers of the combined force, was flown aboard Saratoga *in Fanny Forde's Barracuda to meet Captain Cassady and his officers, and was received with full ceremony.*

A 'Cavour' battleship sunk at Taranto by the Swordfish of HMS Illustrious.

Bombing of HMS Illustrious *in Valletta Harbour. The* Illustrious *can be seen head on under the crane in the centre of the photo. Reports claim only one hit in this raid.*

HMS Illustrious *entering Grand Habour, Malta with Eastern Fleet at anchor.*

Restored and made fit for service again, heading to join the fleet.

A Swordfish being prepared on deck lift.

HMS Illustrious, *sailing into the wind with one Swordfish and another on the approach.*

HMS Illustrious, *with a Fulmar waiting for take off.*

A Swordfish being waved down on to the deck of HMS Illustrious.

Unicorn, Queen Elizabeth, Illustrious *and* Valiant *as seen from* Renown *in the Red Sea, when the Indian Ocean forces were being strengthened with the arrival of modern ships to replace the 'Royal Sovereigns'.*

The hastily assembled East Indies Fleet backed off from battle it could not win in April 1942. Seen here the Warspite, Royal Sovereign *and* Revenge *with carrier* Illustrious.

The landings in the Mediterranean at Sicily and Salerno were covered by powerful British fleets but the Italians failed to appear. Here the Valiant *losens off a few frustrated savoes astern of the* Illustrious *while on patrol.*

A deck landing officer guides an aircraft about to land on HMS Illustrious *with bats, (reflectors with lamps).*

The deck landing officer on Illustrious *is giving a 'Roger' (aircraft is OK for height and line-up) to the pilot of a Grumman Marlet. DLCOs were responsible for safe landing procedures by giving visual instructions to pilots.*

By May 1942, HMS Illustrious *was on operations against Vichy French forces in Diego Suarez Madagascar, and remained in the Indian Ocean from May 1942 until January 1943, where she undertook further operations against Madagascar in September 1942. She undertook a refit in the UK between February-June 1943 then returned to the Mediterranean between August-November 1943 where she took part in the Salerno landings in September 1943.*

A Fulmar landing on the deck of HMS Illustrious.

Stretton.

Meanwhile, Eric Rogers had made a wheels-up landing on the beach outside Hoylake golf course. The ATS were camping on the golf course at the time and he was soon surrounded By a crowd of girls in khaki. Lunch in the ATS officers' mess followed, and Eric was just making himself comfortable in an easy chair with a liqueur and a big cigar when one of the girls who was looking out of the window happened to remark casually:

'Looks like. being a high tide today.'

Eric nearly swallowed his cigar. Rushing down to the beach, he saw his Corsair with water, lapping gently at the cockpit.

There was nothing else for it ATS nothwithstanding, he took off his trousers and waded out to the aircraft. Climbing up into the cockpit, he removed the armour plating from behind the seat, fished in the radio compartment and removed a cache of loot which be had brought from America. The ATS were then treated to the spectacle of a Royal Naval officer in his underpants wading towards them up the beach with his arms full of wrist-watches and nylons. It was a wonder he was not mobbed on the spot.

At Stretton they were all given a week's leave while airscoops were fitted to their Corsairs in an effort to remove the tendency for carbon monoxide fumes to seep back into the cockpit. The opportunity was also taken to fit homing beacon sets for carrier work and to standardise important fittings by putting in British radio and oxygen equipment.

They returned from leave, anxious to know if there had been any word about their future.

There had, and Monk had got it.

'Well, leave's over and we're all going to have to work like a slave from now on,' he announced, bursting into the squadron office. 'We're going to the *Illustrious* in a matter of days!'

As it turned out, Norman did not join the ship until most of the others were aboard.

It was Boxing Day at Macrihanish, Scotland, 1943, cold, bright and crisp. Norman Hanson's head was clear, his mind sharp – thanks to some agonising self-discipline on Christmas Day.

That afternoon they loafed around the squadron office, all a trifle heavy-hearted with apprehension. 'My first deck landing for eighteen months,' thought Norman fearfully, 'and only six logged altogether!'

He himself had only just recovered from an attack of bronchitis contracted at Stretton, and was late joining the ship. By this time the rest of his squadron had done their qualifying deck landings aboard the escort carrier *Slinger*, and had joined *Illustrious*.

Norman was discharged from sick quarters on Christmas Eve.

Waiting for the bus at Campbeltown to take him to Macrihanish, where the squadron had flown from Stretton, he heard the droning of aircraft overhead, looked up and saw the Corsairs of his squadron above him on their way to *Illustrious*.

At Macrihanish he met Dickie Cork, Wing Leader of *Illustrious'* new 15th Royal Naval Fighter Wing, comprising the two Corsair squadrons 1830 and 1833.

'The best thing to cure bronchitis is to get in a Corsair and fly,' said Cork. 'Up you go, cobber!'

Norman flew that morning, wondering as he did so how the rest of 1833 had fared in their first deck landings aboard their new ship.

In point of tact they had got aboard without breaking anything. But they did so practically amidst the wreckage of 1830. For the other squadron, landing-on had been painful.

First they had watched their CO, Brian Fiddes, skid off the flight deck and plunge to his death. This was a terrible sight for the inexperienced young pilots, and a nerve-shaking example. It was not entirely surprising that the next few men crashed their Corsairs all over the ship in various ugly attitudes of failure.

It was a performance which was being repeated by newly-formed Corsair squadrons of the US Navy. In fact the problem had now come to a head, as the rate of casualties among student pilots doing their operational deck-landing training on Corsairs had reached alarming heights.

And they went on mounting until Chance-Vought's emergency 'Programme Dog' removed the ugly bouncing characteristics of the landing struts. From this point the 'U-birds' went from strength to strength, for the remainder of the war they did splendid work with both the US and Royal Navies, In all, nineteen Fleet Air Arm squadrons were equipped with them and nearly two thousand Corsairs issued to the Royal Navy.

But that small group of British airmen waiting at Macrihanish on Boxing Day, 1943, could not see so far into the future. All they could do was to 'twitch' apprehensively as they imagined the hours immediately ahead and the worst that they could bring. *Their* Corsairs had not been immunised.

Only the Fighter Wing Leader, Dickie Cork, who was a tough young veteran of the Battle of Britain and a crack naval pilot, appeared cool and collected. Norman was still shaky from the aftermath of his spell in sick quarters. The other four pilots were 'survivors' of 1830 squadron who had been waved off on that day of catastrophe and sent back to Macrihanish for more ADDL's.

Just before they were due to take off, fhe Commander (Operations) of *Illustrious*, Commander Shaw, handed Norman a letter to give to Commander (Flying) when he got aboard.

'You're optimistic, aren't you, sir?' said Norman.

'My dear fellow' said Shaw, 'I always try to look on the bright side.'

'Well, I hope you've got a copy of this, sir,' said Norman,

Then Shaw briefed them for the short flight.

Illustrious was out in the Firth, cruising somewhere to the south of Ailsa Craig. They were given a course to steer and the R/T call-signs. Then Dickie Cork gave them their order of landing on.

'So let's go,' he said cheerfully, '- and make it good!'

Out on the desolate field of Macrihanish the Pratt and Whitneys roared out lustily as they started up, propellers flinging out the familiar vortices of rainbow vapour. Then they were lumbering off like six huge beetles zig-zagging their way round the perimeter track to the duty runway.

Check-off list – full revs; flaps up; six degrees starboard rudder, zero elevator trim; booster main stage; hydraulic pressure 1,200. Everything OK.

There goes Dickie Cork, now, tail up already, flashing down the runway. Now an 1830 machine. Now my turn.

Tail wheel locked; auto-rich mixture; inter-cooler, oil coolers and cowling gills shut; harness locked. Right!

The gentle ticking-over melts into a massive, roaring crescendo as you push the throttle slowly open and two thousand horse-power hurls the Corsair down the runway. Two slight bumps and she comes unstuck.

Tuck the undercart up and turn to port, looking for the Wing Leader. Bank over to join up, pull the throttle back to climbing boost and the revs sink back to 2,200. Up on the leader now. Ease gently into the number three position on Dickie's port side, settling down to a short spell of close formation flying. Out over the sea again now, still turning back over the Mull. There's number four just gliding into position to port. We roar over Campbeltown at 1,500 feet and faced out into the Forth.

Now, after what seems like only minutes, Dickie Cork signals 'starboard echelon!' Slide slowly under him and number two, and take up the new position.

And suddenly – there she is down there, a tiny shape, a beautiful ship on a silver sea. The little steel grey rectangle of her flight deck appears just below the rising and falling wing-tip of Dickie's aircraft. She seems motionless, so far below – *Illustrious*, our home, and our destiny.

She's turning into wind now. Her wake is like a curved ridge of snow across a heaving grey tableland.

There's R/T chatter in the helmet like a hundred mad parrots, No time to listen – too busy going over the landing-on drill.

The Wing Leader jerks his head back once or twice. Okay, pull back the throttle and lose height.

There's the starboard side of the ship, huge and cliff-like, a wall of steel. Cork gives me 'wheels down, hook down' signal, then breaks away to port Number two follows.

I'm next. Round to port, chasing Tiddles, who is a quarter of a mile ahead.

Down flaps. Steady now – not the lot yet! Down to three hundred feet. Get the speed down a few knots.

Abreast of the bows now, flying down the port side. Now she's level with the stern.

Here goes! Turn into port. *Now* full flaps. Up revs to 2,400 and a hit more boost.

There's 'Roger' from Johnny, the batsman. What speed? Christ! Ninety! Too bloody fast! There, that's better – about eighty-two. Hold it at that.

Roger, Roger, all the way. Bit more speed, eh? Okay, how's that? The stern, the round-down rush in, the deck beneath me now....

CUT!... Johnny's paddle whips across his body. Chop the throttle back, freeze on the stick and hold her there.

There! A bump, a jerk. Hooked, by God! And a beauty! Johnny's grinning like an ape.

Unhook now and taxi forward up the deck. Faster – three more to get aboard yet.

As his Corsair crosses them, the wire barriers clang into the vertical position again, ready to stop tbe next machine should it bounce and miss the arrester wires. But they all get aboard safely.

As he slows up to fold his wings, Norman hears the voice of Commander (Flying) over the deck speakers. He looks ahead at the great bridge island towering up on the starboard side, and the vast expanse of the flight deck ahead of him – so different from the narrow little deck of the old *Argus*, the only carrier he has touched down on before. *It's all a dream – something out of a movie.*

But the aircraft handler, crossing his wrists to tell Norman to cut his engine, is real enough. The deck he jumps down to is genuine, rock-thick armour plating, a solid grey plateau, scarred and oily.

No, this is not imagination, but hard, hard fact. I've got there at last. I'm a carrier fighter pilot.

CHAPTER SIX

A Jutland Wind

At 2115 on December 30th, with extra lashing on the aircraft in the deck park for'd, they glided slowly out through the Clyde boom defence, in the company of the smaller carrier *Unicorn* and several destroyers. Those who had so confidently predicted Norway and the *Tirpitz* were soon disillusioned.

On New Year's Day, 1944, *Illustrious*, instead of sighting the outer guard of the Norwegian islands, stood out into the wide Atlantic, somewhere to the sou'west of the westermost point of Eire.

The Atlantic was quite kind to the new sailors. The ship dipped and rolled gently in a choppy, but not a particularly heavy sea. There was no flying, and the airmen spent most of their time groping their way awkwardly round the ship, getting acquainted with the work of the other departments, feeling very much spare hands as they did so, yet fortified with the knowledge that but for them and their machines this great aggregation of men and metal would have no meaning.

The, solid iron and steel they trod was really the bricks and mortar of a fortress, a great floating castle which sent its fighting-men to sortie against the enemy with bomb, bullet and torpedo. She was a moving outpost, a steel city following a chosen track across the endless plains of the sea.

Within this steel city, living together like a normal tribe, two thousand men worked and kept watch, graded in rigid degrees of rank and function. Besides the pilots, observers and air gunners, there were the squadron ground crews whose job it was to keep the machines in the air – the mechanics who watched over airframes and engines, electrics and guns, keeping them fit for fighting with. These men had one of the roost exacting jobs on board. Their intricate, highly responsible work kept them hard at it in the hot, oily, airless metal box of the hangar.

The base of the great pyramid that was the ship's company was formed by the 'fish-heads', the men who were purely and simply sailors – the executive officers who ran the ship and kept her about her business, the engineers and stokers who drove her, the seamen, signalmen, coders and gunners, cooks, butchers, bakers and sick bay 'times', the stewards and wireless mechanics and the 'in-between' – the ratings of the flight-deck party, who manhandled the aircraft and kept the flight deck efficiently, spotted.

All these, and more, there were inside this great steel shell. Each had his job and was responsible for some part of the ship's efficiency and well-being. But each one, too, was an individual, a man, who had been, perhaps, civilian or professional seaman, clerk or labourer, farmer or accountant, shopkeeper or actor – even a poet. In fact, it was a Fleet Air Arm poet, Hugh Popham, then a young fighter pilot, who best describes the great floating microcosm that is an aircraft-carrier.

'Under the flat, grey, armoured deck,' he writes from *Illustrious* on the eve of Salerno:

'The stuffy intricacies of a ship:
office and workshop,
hangar, galley, mess,
turret and engine-room,
linked, labyrinthine, by lit corridors,
away from sunshine, loud with dynamic hum,
fed air by shaft and fan.
Within me throb and charter of her hull,
island-compact, surrounded by
the limited blue saucer of the sea,
lonely as cities built upon a hill,
life is patterned in an unsure routine.'

It was this 'unsure routine' that Norman Hanson and the other pilots of 1833 and 1830 now began to learn.

Norman shared a cabin with Bash Munnoch, the Middlesbrough boy and ex-Marine, who had been on board somewhat longer than the Senior

Pilot and was more familiar with the layout of the ship. With Bash he threaded his way through the hot, reverberating steel hive of *Illustrious* – the starboard passage; the great box of the hangar, with the flight deck for a lid, in which Corsairs and Barracudas stood dove-tailed together, wings folded, silent and cold as yet; the squadron offices and stores; the matdots' mess decks; the sick bay; the chapel; the main galley; the parachute-packing room. Most intriguing of all, they explored the bridge island, with its Fighter Direction Office full of phones and switches, the Air Operations Room and Plot, compass platform and signal deck, the windswept vantage point of 'Flyco' – the perch above the deck of Commander (Flying) – and the holy ground of the Admiral's bridge.

There was another, a cherished place, on the bridge island structure, which they had already got to know during working up.

'*They gave me a Corsair to beat up the Fleet,*' went me rhyme, '*polished off* Nelson *and* Rodney *a treat;*
Forgot all the masts that stuck up on Formid,
And a seat in the Goofers was worth twenty quid'.

If, for *Formid*, you read *Illustrious*, you have the 'Goofers Platform' where Norman and the others were to spend much time. One Fleet Air Arm pilot has described it thus:

'At the after-end of the island superstructure of our large Fleet carriers of the *Illustrious* class there is a clear bit of deck where, by some oversight. My Lords have omitted to put some gun or other warlike implement. This is known as "The Goofers Platform" or "The Goofers". This platform was where we – for all Naval Air Arm types are ardent goofers – foregathered to watch other poor characters landing. Each and every landing is closely watched and criticised. A running commentary usually accompanies it....

"'He's too ruddy fast.... Get your nose up, man.... What the hell is Bats playing at?... He'll have to go round again.... Oh, lovely landing.... Ruddy good batsman, old Sandy...."

'It is like watching a cricket match. We could all have played the stroke better than the man at the crease.'

The Goofers was not in use at present, but there would be many times in the months ahead when the audience in this, the best part of the house, would look down upon scenes of peril and tragedy.

Meanwhile a friendly warrant officer took Norman on a tour of the engine and boiler rooms, A gunnery lieutenant introduced him to the workings of a 4.5-inch twin turret, a multiple pom-pom and an Oerlikon. Johnny Hastings, the junior batsman, unravelled for him the enigmas of arrester wires, crash barriers, catapults and fire-fighting equipment.

The two Corsair squadrons had been increased in size by now. Originally ten aircraft and pilots per unit, they now had fourteen each. The extra pilots and planes had come from 1831 squadron, which had been broken up and distributed between 1830 and 1833. This now gave each squadron three nights of four machines each, with two more aircraft and pilots as spares to enable odd pilots to be rested.

Of the four new men in 1833, Monk's circus, two were New Zealanders, Ken Seebeck and Matt Barbour; two were English, Joe Vickers from Southport and Alan Booth, a Yorkshireman from West Kirby. Alan Booth turned out to be one of the best pilots in the squadron, sharing that honour with the absent-minded Gordon Aitken, who was anything but absent-minded when it came to flying an aeroplane.

The squadron was sub-divided into three flights. Red, White and Blue.

The CO himself led Red Flight, with young Eric Rogers as his number two, Johnny Baker, the big Canadian, as number three, and Steve Starkey number four.

Blue was Bash Munnoch's squad, and he had a strong team in Stan Buchan, who had replaced Peter Builder, Alan Booth and Joe Vickers.

Norman had White Flight. His wingman was New Zealander Neil Brynildsen, with Gordon Aitken, son of a Ceylon tea planter, and Reggie Shaw from London completing the Senior Pilot's team. The four of them were about as varied a selection of young Britishers as you could find.

They were all of them, the whole squadron, very young and very keen. Norman himself, with his twenty-nine years, felt a bit avuncular when he watched them gathered in eager groups, talking Corsair shop or laughing together with a roar of youthful high spirits not unmixed with a certain nervous tension.

Slowly they all began to learn the routine of the ship. The CO himself took them, four at a time, on a series of conducted tours. He was also quick to see that each man should become familiar and identify himself with his own personal aircraft. To this end, he made each one put on overalls and take an active interest whenever an overhaul was being conducted on his machine, a practice which was uncommon in the Royal Navy and absolutely unknown in the RAF.

They were shown over the entire ship, right down to the propeller shafts turning in their oily tunnels. They had lectures on signals, fire control and damage control. They spent hours standing by in the 'ready room', the AOR, under the bridge, or 'at readiness' in the cockpit, getting pins-and-needles in the bottom. Luckily the sea remained fairly smooth, and they were spared the ultimate horror of heaving their hearts up in the grey Atlantic.

It *was* a trifle rough, however, on the day they joined the battle fleet They rendezvoused in mid-ocean with their battle group – at first only a far-away, winking signal lamp in the murk of a January Atlantic day, then, slowly looming up across the waste of ocean, three great steel-grey monsters, *Valiant*, *Queen Elizabeth* and *Renown*.

It was a great moment for the youngsters. For the first time they were port of a British battle fleet. A Jutland wind blew across their faces that day.

How magnificent the battlewagons looked that afternoon, swaying at eighteen knots through a dirty, choppy swell, the spray flying up from their bows as they bit deep into the ocean. Norman stored away this picture to remember in his old age – if he should ever live to reach it.

Shortly after this the Barracudas started flying anti-submarine patrols and exercises, shuttling to and fro between *Illustrious* and *Unicorn*.

It was on one of these exercises that the Barracudas lost one of their number. Hanson recorded in his diary:

'3.1.44.

'Three days out and we had a casualty. The Barracuda boys were out and about again, using *Unicorn* as a filling-up station, and returned to us at about 1730. One, unfortunately, ditched about 1600 and the driver, a pleasant, quiet cove called Morgan, was drowned.

'Our first – and last, I hope – casualty. (Eternal optimism.)

'4.1.44.

'I spoke too soon. Awakened very early mis morning by two loud "crumps": later proved to be the d/c's of a Barracuda which dived into the drink when his engine cut clean on take-off. Pilot – Wallwork – "looker" and TAG all killed. 847 are having a grim time.'

Once through the Straits and they were in fine weather. Deck hockey became a popular amusement and the soon firmly established *Illustrious* custom of sing-songs round the piano – with Norman playing – began in the evenings.

But the serious side of things began to occupy mem more and more. They all had additional ship and squadron duties to perform. Norman, as Senior Pilot, was responsible for the maintenance of all the squadron's machines, in close co-operation with Chief Madison. Ken Seebeck was Armaments Officer for 1833 – he had to see that all the machine-guns were in working order. The .5's were part of a very complicated mechanical chain. Although, generally speaking, fired electrically, the first round in each gun had to be charged hydraulically, operated by a knob in the cockpit. Ken had the squadron electrical mechanics under him to see to such vital parts as the solenoids for me firing mechanisms and the complex electrical circuits.

Alan Booth looked after squadron stores, which meant the supervision of all kinds of spares and the responsibility for their issue and return. Records had to be checked periodically and such valuable pieces of equipment as testing generators (for electrical circuits) and the gear used for removing Corsair propellers had always to be accounted for promptly. Even when Norman smashed his naval-issue wrist-watch he reported the loss to Booth, who had to obtain Monk's authorisation to issue a new one.

There were various jobs of this kind, one of the most important among them being that of Squadron Adjutant, who looked after the assorted reports and returns necessary to the supervision of squadron strength and personnel. Steve Starkey handled all this paper work, as well as coping with the less onerous job of keeping the Squadron Line Book up to date.

They were also allotted duties in me defence of the ship. Norman, for example, had to act as captain of a multiple pom-pom, should the need arise.

But before they had been in the Mediterranean many days they started flying.

Over the blue waters off the North African coast, white buildings ashore gleaming distantly in the sun. They took off and climbed into the skies that had seen so many savage air battles, where *Illustrious* had fought so bravely in the past.

Their baptism was lively. On one sortie tfaey met some Free French Airacobras from Maison Blanche Airfield in Algiers. Some happy Corsair boy pressed his firing button and the Airacobras fled – *á toute vitesse*.

Then Reggie Shaw, the young Londoner in Hanson's flight, got into trouble. Making a ragged approach, he lost sight of the deck, hit a turret on the post side aft – nearly killing Bats on the deck, – and carried away one of his undercarriage legs. He was ordered to fly ashore and land at Maison Blanche. Unfortunately he missed the airfield as well and finally got down by doing a belly landing in a potato patch.

They aviated a lot in the Mediterranean. One young pilot omitted an important cockpit check and it killed him.

On the left-hand side of the Corsair's cockpit was a lever which operated the hydraulic system for folding the wings. The pilot selected one of three positions of this lever – 'Spread', 'Stop' or Fold'. For take-off he would select 'Spread' and the wings would unfold into the down position. The pilot men had the choice of leaving the hydraulic lever in 'Spread' or putting it into 'Stop', which blanked off the hydraulic system in the wing from the rest of the machine's hydraulic system and firmly locked the wings down. If he chose to leave it in 'Spread' it was essential to operate a second, manual locking device as well, to secure the wings. Otherwise the hydraulic jacks inside the wings remained dangerously open to the whole hydraulic system of the aircraft.

Many pilots preferred to leave the hydraulic lever in 'Spread' in this way and use the manual lock. This was what the young man meant to do, but flying a Corsair was a complicated business and they were all of them beginners still. Rushing off the deck, he had pushed the hydraulic lever into 'Spread'. *But he forgot to pull the manual lock.*

When he was level with the destroyer screen he decided to pull his undercarriage up. This called for great hydraulic pressure. With the hydraulic system of the wings wide open to the rest of the system, the hydraulic fluid drained straight out of the Jacks in the wings. At a height of eighty feet, he saw his wings fold up and inwards upon him. He went in like a stone and was swallowed up by the sea.

His death brought the threat of danger closer to them all – until the shock was swallowed up in the sweat and blinding heat of the tropics. In the Indian Ocean they did no flying whatsoever for a few days in order to allow modifications and inspections to be brought up to date. The hangar was fantastically hot, a steamy, oily purgatory of sweating victims. One youngster fainted, falling heavily to the steel deck from a scaffolding round the engine of a plane. Throughout these days the routine varied little....

'How are things this morning. Chief? How many serviceable?'

'Thirteen OK, one duff – hydraulic leak on the port under-cart.'

'Um – how-long before she'll be fixed?'

'Well, I've got P/O Lester to give it the once-over. If he thinks it's OK she'll be available shortly after lunch.'

That's how it went these days. Repairs and modifications were the rule. After the ship had left Aden all Corsairs were grounded for a minor 'mod'. There had already been some trouble with the Corsair over carbon monoxide poisoning in the cockpit. Three additional airscoops had already been fitted back at Stretton to try to banish the danger, but exhaust gases were still penetrating the cockpit. Now certain alterations were made at the back of the 'office' in the radio compartment. Cracks were sealed off with tape and the machines pronounced cured.

And so they sweated it out. At least now they knew where they were going. When the ship left Aden the Captain told them that *Illustrious* was to go to Trincomalee in Ceylon to be part of the Eastern Fleet.

Another thing they all had to be thankful for was the increasingly happy atmosphere on board. Some carriers there were whose wardrooms were haunts of prejudice and snobbery. RN salthorses snubbed the RNVR 'Temporary' officers of the air squadrons; Dartmouth cold-shouldered the ex-civilian 'chauffeurs'.

This was not the case aboard *Illustrious*, which was to become widely known as 'the happiest floating hotel in the southern hemisphere' and sometimes as 'the only floating lunatic asylum run by its own inmates'.

A 'happy' ship usually has a good captain to thank, and *Illustrious* was lucky in Captain R L B 'Smiler' Cunliffe. Cunliffe was good for the VR's. He liked them, looked after them and sought their company often. And the pleasantness spread from even higher up, for once more *Illustrious* carried an Admiral, Rear-Admiral 'Clem' Moody, who was himself like an uncle to them, who knew all their Christian names and nicknames. His Air Staff Officer was none other than 'Grubby' Going, the same Going who had once forced on alone to Taranto. He stumped cheerfully up and down the steep iron ladders now on one good leg and one metal one, very much an 'alumnus' of the ship.

Arthur Wallis, the Commander of *Illustrious*, contributed very greatly to the happy atmosphere on board. Those who had known the old *Illustrious* in the days of Boyd and Tuck and Streamline Robertson began to see signs of that old spirit returning that had made her such a happy ship to live in and a taut ship to fight Wallis, perhaps, had a more difficult task than Tuck, for he had a larger and a more varied wardroom to control – one hundred and eighty men comprising officers of all branches of the RN and RNVR as well as three squadrons of energetic young flying-men from Britain and the Dominions. But he handled them all with infinite tact and patience and made *Illustrious* the happiest ship in the Eastern Fleet. 'Wings', too, Ian Sarel, was a real friend and messmate, always ready to laugh with them, always sympathetic to their problems, a man who got things done by the affection he inspired rather than by hard discipline.

Commander (Ops) Terence Shaw, a big, black-bearded man, was just such another. It was his job to work out plans for air operations and to correlate information obtained afterwards by 'de-briefing' air crews. Unfortunately, he was not with the ship very long. When he left he was greatly missed. Another senior officer of ship who was a great friend to the young airmen was Commander (E) 'Bud' Newsom. As well as running the engine-room department, Newsom was responsible for the arrester wires and crash barriers. A slip on his part might mean a pilot hurt or killed. His close friends knew that this thought never left his mind, day or night.

Perhaps the best friend and mentor to the Corsair boys we as Dickie Cork. Dickie was already famous, almost a legend, in the Fleet Air Arm. He had been one of the RN pilots seconded to the RAF for the Battle of Britain. As a Sub-Lieutenant hs had been Bader's wingman and had acquitted himself after that peerless fighter's own heart. ,Now he was a Lieutenant-Commander and the Fighter Wing Leader of *Illustrious*. He was a tall, very good-looking young man, full of charm and friendliness, Most impressive of all, he was a natural leader with that priceless gift of command which shows itself in friendliness without familiarity, and thus achieves firm, unquestioned authority. Dickie was a superb pilot into the bargain. Aeroplanes were his life blood and to show yourself as keen as he was about them was to become a friend at once.

Another matey soul was 'Fanny' Fords, CO of 810 Barracuda squadron. Forde had been one of Hale's bomber boys at Taranto, so he knew the old ship well, even with her face-lift. His squadron knew they would have to live up to Taranto. He and Dickie Cork were always in great demand at parties for their large repertoire of West Indian calypsos.

Of the Corsair men, the majority mixed well together. The CO kept very much to himself, although he had lately struck up a friendship with Johnny Baker, partly on the basis of their both being teetotallers in the midst of a crowd who drank their whisky clear – and their gin at tuppence-ha'penny a tot.

The CO of 1830, squadron was now Mike Tritton, an Old Etonian, who had been brought in to take over the squadron when Brian Fiddes was killed. Tritton was a young Lieutenant-Commander, who had been one of the very early RNVR volunteers to join the Fleet Air Arm. He was already a distinguished officer and had seen much active service from late 1939 onwards. His Distinguished Service Cross had been hard earned in the desperate battles fought over Malta and Sicily when he had flown from the torn airstrips of the George Cross island in the epic days of 'Faith, Hope and Charity'.

Although young in years, Mike had an air of quiet authority about him and was far from bring a normal fighter 'type'. Unlike so many, he did not smack of the 'trade' he was in: there was no oil on his jacket or green salt on his flying badge, and he was never known to shoot a line, in spite of having material for many. He could never be seen performing extravagant aerobatics, but was a fine, safe pilot who knew his job thoroughly.

'Can't stand being upside down, old boy,' was his favourite way of closing somebody else's line shoot.

In the wardroom his Etonian reserve kept him on the outside of the rowdier circles and was mistaken by some for an anti-social attitude. He did take a lot of getting to know, it was true. but those who took the trouble found him a very real and genuine person, a young man who had absorbed the public-school tradition of leadership and who apparently fulfilled that part of his job naturally and instinctively. This easy assumption of the burden of command was, however, rather more apparent than real in one direction, for Mike, in spite of his air of equanimity, cared far more than he would ever admit for his pilots, and others could see more easily than he knew how deeply losses always hurt him.

His air of command and quiet mastery of the job were accepted immediately by all his young British pilots, but were not obvious enough qualities to impress the usual Dominion type of pilot. Perhaps he did not shout loud enough for some of them or act the tough fighter boy. Whatever it was, Mike's type and their type did not hit it off, and he preferred, as a general rule, not to have Colonials in 1830.

There were one or two exceptions, notably Bud Sutton, who had been Brian Fiddes' senior pilot, a breezy 'Aw the hell!' kind of Canadian, and 'Pop' Quigg, a firebrand from New Zealand. His best pilot and right-hand man was Percy Cole, an Englishman, who became his senior pilot.

The congeniality of the wardroom made up for some of the less pleasant things that happened aboard – the small humiliation, for example, of 1833's pilots on being ordered into the hangar to belt up ammunition, the nagging fret and sweat over the aircraft and the sticky, stinking heat over it all.

Then at last they neared Ceylon. Over the blowers one evening came the warble of a bosun's call. Then:

'D'ye hear there! D'ye hear there! The ship will arrive on the coast of Ceylon during the night and will fly off aircraft of all squadrons before proceeding to Trincomalee. Squadron commanders are requested to report to Commander (Flying) in the AOR.'

The CO's duly reported to the Air Operations Room, where Wings told them that arrangements had been made for them to go to China Bay. The Corsairs would move on later to Minneriya, a rattier primitive airfield in the centre of Ceylon.

It was all a great deal more serious now. There was a definite feeling of impending action in the air. The Japs were only just across the water.

Minneriya was certainly primitive, nothing much more in fact than a jungle strip surrounded by bamboo native huts. The jungle lay all around them and all sorts of unpleasant wild life abounded. One young midshipman of 1830 had just landed, when he sensed something or somebody looking at him, close behind. He glanced quickly over his shoulder and saw a monkey sitting on his tail, making faces at him. A near panic was the result when somebody hung a dead snake in the showers. Scorpions, too, helped to make life exciting.

They flew bard and often, practising 'ADDL's' and formation flying, gunnery and fighter tactics. March found them embarked again. Excitement was in the air. When would it be – and where?

There was another tragedy on March 10th, when a Barracuda failed to pull out of its dive and hurled headlong into the sea, disintegrating frighteningly on impact. 'A most understandable quietness in the wardroom this evening,' wrote Norman. Norman himself had had to make an emergency landing late in the afternoon with a complete hydraulic failure. He was lucky. 'Walked away from it,' he wrote. It was a black day, but worse was to follow:

> Saturday, March 11th, 1944.
> 'I thought yesterday had enough but, my God! Today was ghastly. Landed on, just after Don (Hadman, 1830) had gone into the barrier. Taxied up to the forward lift and heard the most appalling crash behind me. Jumped out as the lift started to go down and saw an aircraft...'

It was a Corsair, whose he did not know, lying where it had smashed down across the top of number two pom-pom, abreast of the bridge. The plane's tilted nose, and its guns, pointed across the deck at the compass platform. He could see the pilot, unconscious, perhaps dead, slumped forward in the cockpit.

For a second everything seemed to hang still, aghast and irresolute. Then one or two figures detached themselves from the stillness, starting a frenzy of activity around the danger point of the crashed plane. Others hung back, forbidden by order to approach the crash. The Corsair hung there, ominously still.

Norman saw three figures jump on to the wing and grope for the pilot. Ron Alcock, the flight-deck doctor, on one wing, and a sick-bay chief petty officer on the other side, ripped at his straps. A third man jumped astride the hump of the plane just behind the cockpit and reached down under the motionless man's armpits to drag him clear.

For a second the tableau focused and burned sharp on Norman's mind – three men jerking like figures in a puppet ballet around the slumped body of the pilot.

There had been so sign of further danger yet, no spark or lick of flame, just motionless metal and a lifeless man.

But now, without warning, a terrible thing happened. At the heart of the rescue, in the very face of the rescuers, the plane's main petrol tank exploded.

There was a roar and a great gush of flame. The horrified watchers saw, in a second, the Chief killed outright, hurled to the deck, the Doctor crumple, badly burned, and, most terrible of all, the third rescuer, all aflame, flung into the sea like a torch.

The Corsair was a great firework in an instant, burning and exploding in its death throe's. Bullets from its guns sprayed the bridge. Fire glowed, insatiable, inside it, devouring plane and pilot; mercifully, the pilot had been killed outright on the first crash into the turrets and felt nothing now. Fire-fighters of the flight-deck party sprayed the flames with quenching foam. Some they put out, but the fire inside they could not quench.

They could not save the men at the pom-pom who were killed and burned, or the young sailors trapped by a flood of burning oil and petrol in the ready-use lockers and burned to death there.

There was one consolation. The crash itself was an appalling thing, but such is the cruel-kindness of fate that the pilot's death was the source of life to some of his messmates.

Three Barracudas, their radios all out of action, had got out of touch with the ship and were lost. They had almost given up hope when on the horizon they caught sight of a thin, faint column of smoke shot through with a needle of fire. This tree of flame, one man's funeral pyre, was a landmark to them and brought them home.

After this crash, some of the pilots began to consider themselves survivors. The flight deck felt like a battlefield. The Barracudas particularly had had a number of ugly disasters. They had lost two more crews in the Mediterranean, blown up in the water by their own depth-charges after a forced landing.

The tragic succession of fatal crashes had shaken the Corsair pilots somewhat. In spite of the pleasant atmosphere aboard ship, all was not well with them. The two squadrons did not blend as well as they could have done, and 1833 was not a happy unit. There was constant trouble of some kind with the Corsairs, usually in the shape of barrier prangs, and a general feeling behind it all that the sooner they had some definite action the better. The pattern that had begun to shape was disintegrating. Time and uncertainty were sawing at their nerves, morale was fraying at the edges.

One answer to the problem of morale arrived on board in the person of the new flight-deck medical officer.

Bob Ellison had actually been specially trained to help air-crews cope with the problems that the young men of *Illustrious*' air group had now begun to face.

He joined the ship at Colombo on a Sunday morning, with last-mmute misgivings as he climbed aboard the great bulk of the carrier and saw the Rear-Admiral's flag wearing idly in the faint breeze that sidled in from the

Indian Ocean.

He need not have worried. Up on deck he was met by Arthur Wallis, beaming a welcome and twinkling for all he was worth. The Commander took him by the arm and led him below to the wardroom.

Bob had come aboard at gin time – the best possible time to meet naval officers socially. Wallis ushered him in and he found himself on the fringe of a vast crowd of RN and RNVR types, laughing, chattering, standing or sprawling in armchairs, clutching gins, and giving every impression of geniality. Wallis started introducing him round the wardroom, and his first snap impression of friendliness and informality deepened. In the buzz of chatter there was a lightness and aliveness that he had not noticed in shore stations. There was a marked casualness about, everybody. No one went out of his way to impress. Sometimes, however, an inflection of the voice or a preoccupied stare made him wonder whether there might not be disturbed currents underneath, this smiling surface.

There was a preponderance of 'straight stripers' in the senior ranks, he noticed, but an enormous majority of 'wavy navy's' lower down the scale, particularly among the aircrews. He met quiet, serious Mike Tritton, the young CO of one of the Corsair squadrons, and liked him at once. In fact they were all very likeable, particularly another north-countryman he was introduced to, Norman Hanson of 1833, the other fighter squadron. The two of them got on well from the start and soon struck up a firm friendship. Each liked the other's informality and good nature, each admired the other's underlying conscientiousness and enthusiasm for the flying game. The tall, lean pilot thought the doctor, with a concern part professional, part friendly, seemed more than a little preoccupied behind his steady smile, and there were lines of strain in his face.

The diagnosis was accurate enough, and there was a very good reason for the strain. Hanson was another young man to whom things had been happening fast of late.

Only a day or so before he had had to take a Corsair out to the 'workshop' carrier *Unicorn* for repairs. He was sitting in the aircraft preparing to taxi out and take off, when Dickie Cork hailed him.

'Hello, Hans, where are you off to?' shouted the Wing Leader.

'Taking this cab to *Unicorn* for a mod,' he yelled back, Dickie came up and climbed on to the wing.

'When are you coining back?" he asked.

'Oh, I don't know, sir – some time after lunch I should think, or whenever I can got a lift.'

'All right. It's just that there might be some interesting news for you when you get back, that's all. So long.'

Norman thought no more of it but took off, headed out to sea and shortly afterwards landed aboard *Unicorn*. He had lunch aboard, and in the afternoon Johnny Cox, of 847 Squadron brought him back to China Bay in a Barracuda.

When he got back he went into the big marquee which served as a squadron office to make the customary report of his return to the CO. Monk was not there, however, only Bash Munnoch.

'Any idea where Charlie Orange is. Bash?'

'He's on board ship,' said Bash. 'A Marine came here about half-eleven with a chit for him to report to the Skipper.'

'What about?'

'I don't know. He's been a hell of a long time though.'

Norman shrugged. 'Have you heard what time we're embarking?' He knew *Illustrious* was leaving that night.

'1730.'

'We'd better organise the blokes to get aboard the seaplane tender at that time, then.'

In due course they assembled on the quay. In came the seaplane tender which was to take them out to the ship.

There were quite a number for embarkation – and one to disembark.

It was Monk. What is more, he was dressed up smartly in his blues and surrounded by luggage. With a grin on his face he jumped out of the boat and grabbed Norman's hand.

'Well, cheerio, Hans, all the best to you. Look after the kids.'

The Senior Pilot was flabbergasted.

'Where the hell do you think you're going?'

'UK'

"What, now?'

'Right away. Well, I've got to rush. So long, be seeing you.'

'So long....' He never saw him again.

He went back to *Illustrious* in a daze, and next morning they sailed at 0730. Towards the middle of the morning the Captain sent for him.

'You know Monk has left the ship?'

'Yes, sir, I met him on the jetty.'

'What are we going to do about it?'

'Find another CO, sir.'

'Have you ever run a squadron before?'

'No, sir.'

'Think you can run this one?'

It was a shock, but he had no need to think twice.

'I'm sure I can, sir.'

'Right, you're on. Start now.'

And that was all. In a glow of surprise and rising elation he went to see Dickie Cork. The interview was less than brief.

'You know the things I want you to do, Hans. All right – off you go and do them. Oh... and move into Monks cabin forthwith, of course.'

Now the real impact hit him. He had a squadron. The lad from Whitehaven had a squadron – a Royal Navy fighter squadron. *Pinch me, and I'll wake up.*

It would mean promotion, too. It would be Lieutenant-Commander Hanson now, or at least in the near future. Something to write – home about – the best bit of news since be got his commission. *A squadron...*

As it turned out the promotion was long delayed, while he was the subject of a steady stream of signals between Rear-Admiral Moody and the Admiralty.

My Lords considered that Lieutenant Hanson lacked the necessary experience for the job. They offered in his stead a choice of three men, one a Hellcat, one a Firefly and one a Seafire pilot. The Admiral replied with some heat that a Corsair squadron, at this moment embarked and in the middle of the Indian Ocean preparing for its first offensive operations needed someone rather more to the point.

He got his way in the end and Norman was eventually 'confirmed' and promoted. But it took. a little time.

And here they were in the middle of the Indian Ocean, a veteran ship but, for the most part, an untried air group, a bunch of young men whose experience so far was of sweat and shocks, and 'bitching about', of crash after fatal crash, of doubt and death. They were young, the youngest barely schoolboys, most of them were inexperienced, few were professional fighting men and none of them were yet complete masters of their temperamental machines. Of the men who would lead them into action, two were 'Temporary' RNVR officers, and one of these was a man who could count his days in command on the fingers of one hand, a young ex-civil servant with no combat experience.

Bob Ellison wondered how they would come out, as he watched them all, so casual, so unworried. It was a casualness, he knew, which was more apparent than real. He felt he would like to tell them, somehow, that he was on their side.

CHAPTER SEVEN

ILLUSTRIOUS AND 'SARA'

Illustrious was at sea with urgent business on hand, heading east across the Indian Ocean, with the other ships of the Eastern Fleet around her.

Soon, with her bows pointing to the Pacific, she drew near to Australia. A scented breeze seemed to be blowing her way from tropical islands scattered like stars across her track.

Also somewhere across her path, so everybody hoped, was a German blockade-runner which the Barracudas would be very interested to find.

But there was another motive for their sortie.

As they approached the western edge of Australia, over the distant horizon like a breath of spring came the Americans. Straight for the British Fleet like John Paul Jones came the great carrier *Saratoga*, the queen of the Pacific.

And as she met *Illustrious* on that bright blue day, history met history face to face, veteran shook hands with veteran. The British ship brought with her Taranto, Salerno, and the Malta convoys, *Saratoga* the glory of Guadalcanal and the Solomons, Rabaul and the Gilberts and Marshalls.

Saratoga, CV-3, affectionately known as 'Sara' by every matelot in the US Fleet, was a unique ship in many ways. Almost the oldest carrier afloat, and certainly the oldest to be operating as one of a fast carrier task force, she was the biggest aircraft-carrier in the world.

She came, this American veteran, from a vast, blue-battlefield where great fleets had already locked together to the death to a score of terrible battles, from a wide ocean where the savage, skilful Japanese still deployed their might, but where the power of the US Navy was surging forward everywhere, the mightiest fleet the world had seen since Jutland. She came from a vast world of water where Mitscher roamed at will with his twelve great carriers of Task Force 58 – less one, now that *Saratoga* had joined with *Illustrious* and the British Eastern Fleet to give the Japanese the left and right of yet another smashing Allied strike.

It was 1145 on the morning of March 27th when the two groups first sighted each other. As 'Sara' and her prancing destroyers, *Fanning*, *Dunlap* and *Cummings*, all veterans of the Pacific war, came up with the British ships, the whole assembly turned in company on to a course which took them back across the Indian Ocean. *Saratoga* had manned ship for the occasion, and the long lines of white-clad sailors looked very smart and seamanlike.

'Our communications signal crew,' wrote Commander Bob Dose, CO of 'Sara's' fighter squadron, 'had been practising British signals and as the two fleets neared, our crews were preparing to raise British signals but the British beat us to it. They raised American signals. We conceded.'

One up to the Limeys.

Then there was an exchange of visits by planes from each carrier.

Admiral Moody, as Admiral Commanding Aircraft Carriers of the combined force, was flown aboard *Saratoga* in Fanny Forde's barracuda to meet Captain Cassady and his officers, and was received with full ceremony.

With the Admiral in the back seat was Johnny Hastings, junior batsman of the British carrier. He was left on board to prevent complications which might otherwise arise over the differences between British and American deck landing signals. Operating procedure in the two navies differed in detail, and, as *Illustrious* and 'Sara' were to work closely together on operations, it was essential that each ship should carry a batsman who knew the other's methods. Royal Navy and US aircraft would be landing on each other's decks from time to time, and if, for example, a Barracuda or Corsair making a dart at 'Sara's' deck were to interpret an American batsman's uplifted paddles as 'Get up *higher!*' he would probably come to an untimely end, for the same signal in US Navy procedure meant 'You're too high! Get *lower*' With Johnny aboard, however, he would know where he was. Shortly afterwards some of *Saratoga*'s SBDs flew aboard *Illustrious* and left behind an American deck landing control officer, as well as several signals officers to help smooth out communications problems.

When Forde brought his Barracuda to rest after an immaculate snagging of the third wire, flight-deck spectators crowded round the British counterpart of their own TBF. Their remarks were not complimentary.

'Jesus!' said one lieutenant. The Limeys'll be building *airplanes* next!'

The next night the *Saratoga's* Douglas Dauntless dive-bombers, the SBDs, were out looking for the suspected German raider. They made a thorough search but sighted nothing and returned to make a perfect land-on in a roaring rainstorm.

The SBDs put up an impressive display, and went on to show me British mat it was'no flash-in-the-pan. A little later on Norman Hanson wrote in his diary:

> Thursday, March 30th, 1944 (at sea, returning to Trincomalee, after meeting *Saratoga*).
>
> '...This afternoon *Sara* shook us solid with a wonderfully co-ordinated dive-bombing attack on a towed target, using eighteen SBDs and twenty F6Fs. Beautifully executed, followed by a snappy land-on *with no prangs!'*

The performance which Norman watched with such admiration had been staged by Air Group 12, comprising the same three squadrons which had performed so well in the recent invasion of the Marshall Islands, when '*Sara*' had done great work covering the landings of the US Marines.

The dive-bombing squadron, VB-12, was a splendid unit of twenty-four SBD-5 Douglas Dauntlesses under Lieutenant-Commander Vincent S Hathorn, US Navy. Commander R G Dose, US Naval Reserve, had the fighter squadron, VF-12 – thirty-six F6F-3 Grumman Hellcats – and the eighteen TBM-1C Grumman Avengers of VT-12 were led by Lieutenant W E Rowbotham, USN, a splendid flier – an officer, incidentally, of Red Indian descent.

It was a crack air group at the peak of its form, and the British pilots knew that they would have to be on their toes if they were to co-operate with the Americans.

One very good reason for their splendid form was their Air Group Commander. On the afternoon following the SBDs' display, he himself flew on board *Illustrious* to pay his respects.

'Who should arrive on board,' wrote Norman, 'but old Jumping Joe!'

Commander J C 'Jumping Joe' Clifton, US Navy, came on board in a Hellcat. The F6F made a perfect touchdown, unhooked and came to a stop. Out jumped a big man with a broken nose and the build of a cruiser-weight champion. He went straight up to the bridge where the Captain was waiting to welcome him on board. Before Cunliffe could offer the usual 'Glad to have you aboard', the Commander had mumped him on me back and got his word in first with a –

'Hiya, Captain, I'm mighty glad to know yuh! Say, you've got a mighty fine little ship here, yes sir!'

Jumping Joe recognised some of the faces he saw aboard the British carrier – the faces of fighter pilots, including Norman Hanson, who had done their initial fighter training under his command at Miami Fighter School two years before. A lot of salt water has flowed for all them since then.

At 0845 on the 31st both carriers flew off aircraft to China Bay. *Illustrious'* Barracudas and Corsairs were joined there by thirty Hellcats, four SBDs and four Avengers from *Saratoga*.

Then the ships entered harbour. That evening *Illustrious* invited the entire air group from the American carrier to a party in the wardroom. In anticipation of the enormous inroads likely to be made upon the ship's store of booze, the bar, normally open at 1745, was not opened on this occasion until three hours later. This was just as well, for a hundred thirsty naval airmen arrived from *Saratoga* – all the thirstier because their own ship was 'dry'.

As soon as their guests arrived aboard, Norman and some of the other Corsair boys became involved in reunions. Not only was Jumping Joe in full-scale attendance, but he had brought with him a crowd of ex-instructors from Miami, all of whom had been there with him when Norman and his pals were under training. Hand-picked by Joe for his squadrons, they obviously accounted for much of the *esprit de corps* and four-zero efficiency of Air Group 12.

There was Willis, a big, husky, jolly individual, and 'Baby' Winterrowd, short, dark, cat-like, a Hellcat pilot out of the top drawer. Baby was dripping, as usual, though the sight of all that liquor cheered him up enormously. There was Red Cassady, a fighter pilot from Illinois, with his fiery, crew-cut hair and pugnacious but jovial face. A husky lad was Red, with a permanent grin that went with one of the kindest hearts in the world. These three, and Charlie 'Moto' Motz, too, from Georgia, had all been Norman's' instructors at one time or another, and the reunion was naturally celebrated with all proper respect. Norman met 'Sara's' fighter leader too. Bob Dose, a tall, dark, lean and rather saturnine-looking pilot. Dose seemed rather reserved and did not open up like the others, though they got to know him better later on.

In all, seven hundred bottles of beer, thirty-six of whisky and a like number of gin were emptied that evening. By the end of the party everybody was about ready to walk up the wall. The Americans returned to their ship eventually, though few of them remembered doing so in the morning.

The exceptions were doubtless those who had decided to dive off the quarter deck of *Illustrious* and swim the two cables back to *Saratoga*. Searchlights on the British carrier were kept busy picking out the swimmers while her boats picked the more uncertain ones out of the water and returned them to their own ship.

The boats were piled to the gun'ls with singing sailors.

'Gee, Commander, I'm sorry,' said an anxious Jumping Joe at the gangway.

'That's quite all right, old boy,' said Arthur Wallis, beaming and twinkling.

'All this racket...' said Joe, gesturing at the boat which was at that moment filling up at the gangway.

'Pay no regard, old boy' said Wallis.

But Jumping Joe wanted to square his boys with the British Navy. He glared down at the boatload of pilots who were at that moment informing Trincomalee that they were all of them 'poor little lambs who have lost our way'.

'Listen, you guys!' he shouted in a bull-like roar and, pointing with a dramatic gesture at the 'scrambled eggs' on his cap, 'I got the lace! Now QUIT IT!... Gee, I really am sorry, Commander....'

Wallis had apparently run out of words, for he merely smiled, albeit a trifle glassily, and sniffed benignly at the gin-laden breeze. Everyone, it seemed, had had a good evening.

The combined fleet spent a fortnight at Trincomalee swinging round the hook, getting to know each other. American sailors took a good look at Ceylon, spending rupees for the first time and collecting souvenirs. High-ranking British officials made many formal visits to *Saratoga* and inspected her and her very trim and seamanlike ship's company. Some visitors from her British 'chummy ship' came to scoff at American ways, particularly the US Navy's fondness for ice-cream. In a very short time, however, the scornful laughter died away and the Eastern Fleet developed an unaccountable taste for the stuff themselves.

Some of the British fliers found a sudden improvement in their creature comforts, due to the generosity of the Americans. They found that their laundry was getting done properly for the first time, thanks to US Navy dhobeying machines, and they smoked nothing now but American cigarettes, obtained in quantity, two hundred per carton, as gifts from their opposite numbers in *Saratoga*. Norman appeared puffing at a new pipe, another gift from Air Group 12.

'Don't you have a pipe, Hans?' Jumping Joe had said. 'Hell, I'll give you one!'

Next day he brought over a brand-new, expensive Dunhill and presented it to his former pupil. That is the kind of man he was.

All in all, this example of Anglo-American co-operation looked as if it would work out. The men were mixing well, particularly the rather less traditionally-minded air groups. The fliers went ashore together and took their sport together, whether it be drinking, chasing long-haired chums or simply swimming in the blue Indian Ocean. The Americas spent a lot of time aboard *Illustrious*, partly for the rum and gin and other liquid fire they were denied on their own ship.

'I dunno,' said one British petty officer, 'but it's bloody funny seein' them gobs gettin' pi-ackered on Nelsons blood. I can see the old bastard *revolvin'* in 'is grave!'

But it wasn't all play during this pleasant fortnight. Both air groups put in some hard practice.

The Corsairs went through an intensive programme of training. Norman's log book shows the extent of the work;

'April 1. Corsair JT 282 – Rolling attacks.
April 2. Corsair JT 2S2 – Patrol and escort formation.
April 2. Corsair JT 282 – Training flight with new pilot.
April 4. Hellcat US Navy 30674 – Local flying.'

The latter was a pleasant exchange flight in one of the current standard US Navy fighters. He found the F6F a wonderfully airworthy machine. Then it was back to the grind of training:

'April 5. Corsair JT 347 – ADDL (Hastings).
April 6. Corsair JT 282 – High cover escort exercise,
April 7. Corsair JT 282 – ADDL (Cunningham),
April 7. Corsair JT 282 – Strafing over ship,
April 10. Corsair JT 371 – Ail test.'

Corsair 371 was a new machine. To get it, Norman had to fly his old machine, 282, from China Bay to Coimbatore, in Madras Province, and make the exchange there. An escort carrier had ferried the new aircraft to Cochin, where it was assembled and taken inland by lorry to Coimbatore, where all new machines were test-flown before being handed over to first-line pilots.

He broke the new Corsair in on an intensified programme of exercises:

'April 11. Corsair 371 – Pre-dawn and dawn formation.
April 11. Corsair 371 – Squadron low and medium cover exercise.

April 12. Corsair 371 – Pre-dawn form-up and formation.
April 12. Corsair 371 – Defence of fleet against Beauforts.
April 13. Corsair 371 – China Bay – *Illustrious*.'

Training 'almost over, they were back aboard ship now. But they still had to do a combined exercise with *Saratoga*. They did this on the afternoon of their return to Illustrious and Norman recorded it thus:

'April 13. Corsair 326 – Abortive attempt at umbrella over *Renown* during X with *Saratoga*,'

The exercise was, indeed, an abortion.

'Due solely, I think,' said Commander Dose, CO of VF-12, 'to a lack of any pre-flight joint briefing, it took us an hour and fifty minutes to accomplish even a semblance of a rendezvous, and by that time the planes were so low on fuel that we could do nothing but return to the ships and land.'

Jumping Joe immediately requested, and was granted, a conference aboard *Illustrious*, which was the senior ship.

When Jumping Joe arrived he jumped, big cigar and all, straight up to Admiral Moody's territory on the flag bridge.

This was hardly accepted British (or American) procedure, but it was typical of Joe, who believed above all in getting thing done.

He then held a meeting, as senior aviator, of all the British pilots, at which he shouted clearly and in precise detail the techniques which all the British and American pilots were hence-forth to use in their joint operations. The meeting was very beneficial. Ideals flowed freely, mostly from behind Jumping Joe's cigar, and the next time they all took off they were able to get together in a little over twenty-five minutes, 'leaving us,' as Commander Dose said, 'the long kgs necessary tor a strike.'

And the strike, the British air group's first, was almost on them. But first came yet another disaster for the Corsairs, a disaster, in fact, for the whole fleet.

On the day after the 'abortive' cffort, a dawn exercise had been scheduled for *Illustrious*. The Corsairs were to take off before dawn, join up and land at China Bay in the first early light.

Wind conditions were more often than not against them in these exercises. The breeze was fickle in the Indian Ocean and changeable.

So it was this morning – Corsairs ranged dimly on deck, and the Captain manoeuvring his ship this way and that in the darkness, sniffing for a breath of wind.

Then he found a breeze of sorts and Dickie Cork, first in the range, opened his throttle and rolled down the deck.

By the time he had reached the bows the wayward wind must have lost interest. He went off shakily with nothing under his wings but the paint. A less experienced pilot than Cork would almost certainly have pranged in the circumstances, and Wings decided it was madness to launch anyone else. Meanwhile Dickie was left circling the ship in the darkness, navigation lights twinkling like small stars. Eventually he was told to land ashore at China Bay and given a course to steer.

'Cheerio, daps – see you ashore,' he crackled over the R/T, and was gone into the blackness. Only his tail light blinked once, faltered and went out, like a star behind a cloud.

A few hours later the ship came into harbour. As soon as she dropped anchor, a launch came alongside and a naval doctor climbed aboard..

In two minutes the buzz was round the ship.

'There's been an accident at China Bay.'

'Know who it is?'

'No, not yet.'

Norman fett a twinge of foreboding. It was Dickie. It *must* be Dickie. He prayed that it was not.

Alas for their hopes – it *was* Dickie Cork. They had lost there gallant Wing Leader.

The details told of a tragic, futile waste.

On the single airstrip at China Bay when Cork arrived over it, another Corsair was waiting to take off. In its cockpit, as it taxied slowly down from the up-wind end of the runway preparatory to turning at the other boundary and taking off into wind, was a young pilot who was about to join *Illustrious* out at sea to do his scheduled six practice deck landings and join the ship.

As Cork arrived over the runway with all his lights on, the other pilot started to taxi. Dickie, impatient to get down, pushed his wheels down and came in to land. With the runway blocked by the Corsair coming in the opposite direction, the RAF controller gave Cork a long 'red' on the Aldis lamp and the Wing Leader promptly picked up his wheels and sheered off.

He came in again, put his wheels down and, naturally, the same thing happened. But Cork, a high-speed man, one of the best pilots ever to climb into a cockpit, for some reason chose to ignore the warning and came in.

The young pilot saw him coming. In his fright and inexperience, instead of braking hard on one wheel and getting off the runway – the jungle would have done him little damage – all he could think of to do was to blink his navigation lights.

The two Corsairs crashed head-on, locked together and exploded in flame. In a few minutes they were nothing but a heap of twisted metal and hot ashes on the runway.

They were buried next morning with full military honours.

With a warm-hearted gesture of respect and comradeship, the American air group turned out to line the route of the funeral procession. Jumping Joe Clifton and many of his boys walked in – the procession itself. They, too, had known and loved Dickie.

But none so deeply as the young pilots of his own ship. It was the night of Friday, April 14th. Dickie Cork was gone. Now the responability of leadership rested squarely upon the shoulders of the two young squadron commanders.

Five days later they were in action, trying to put into practice the things which that peerless flier had taught them – and remembering him as they did so.

The mission was strategical. Sabang was the target, an island lying close to the northern tip of Sumatra.

Sabang was small, but vital. Concentrated there were oil storage tanks, an airfield and a submarine base. The oil went by tanker north to Rangoon, the airfield was a staging point for Japanese aircraft flying into Burma, the submarines were a menace to our shipping. It was high time something was done about Sabang.

The carriers were now going to do it. They could roam and strike at will over an area that would require a hundred airfields to police. And airfields, fixed and vulnerable, gave away their strategic purpose. They are always there for enemy reconnaissance to keep an eye on. A carrier may attack one place and be hitting another, three hundred miles way tomorrow, before the enemy knows what has hit him. No enemy with a long coastline can possibly defend all his vital areas adequately against this kind of flexible offensive.

Illustrious had done this sort of job before in the Mediterranean, and *Saratoga* had done it in the Pacific. Now together they were to initiate just such a mobile offensive in me east, with Sabang the opening phase.

Specific targets on Sabang were the huge oil storage tanks, the airfield, tankers, supply ships and submarines in the harbour, as well as the radar station and power station and sundry targets in the town.

The British Barracudas were to take the power station targets in the town and the go-downs at the water's edge where shipping was thick. The Americans would attack the rest. Above the whole strike Jumping Joe and his flight would hover and co-ordinate the attack in accordance with the fluctuating tide of battle.

1833's Corsairs were laid on to give 810 Squadron's Barracudas close support. 810 was Fanny Forde's circus and together he and Norman worked out the details. The main idea was for the Corsairs to go down with the bombers and make the Japanese ack-ack gunners keep their heads down. What no one allowed for was the fact that Japanese gunners never *put* their heads down. They found that out the hard way. The fighters were to stay with the Barracudas during their way in, flying just above them, then pull away at about three thousand feet on a signal from Forde, and go on ahead to strafe the gunners.

It was the Corsair boys' first op. However, they turned in that night excited but not at all apprehensive. In fact, they were quite eager and light-hearted in their ignorance. They were nervous, but only in the way of high-spirited youngsters before an important rugger match. They anticipated difficulties, but danger and death were somehow not in their happy-go-lucky calculations.

Take-off at 0650 next morning was exciting but uneventful. They'd taken off together many times before and flown across the sea enough in formation for the novelty to have worn a bit thin by now. But they had never yet crossed enemy coast. They sat in their aeroplanes and strained their eyes for Sabang.

When it did appear it wasn't at all the frowning landscape they had expected. Instead, a little green tropical island rose from the silver water and posed seductively against the silken curtain of the pale blue early-morning sky. When the first dirty, black mushroom of flak began to blossom silently above the island, it seemed like sacrilege.

No fighters came up to meet them, so the 1833 boys focused their thoughts and energies intently upon their own job. They nosed over and went down with the Barracudas as planned, keeping above and slightly to the side of the bombers so as to keep the opposition in full view.

'*Now*, Hans!' said Fanny crisply over the R/T, and they poured in the gas and shot ahead.

Norman, in the lead, aimed at the gun flashes appearing above the leading edge of his wings, too excited at first pass to notice details. Then they joined up again. There was a barrage of chatter on the R/T now and from it Nonnan managed to glean that Jumping Joe's wingman, Lieutenant (jg) Dale 'Klondike' Klahn, with whom Joe had flown nearly five hundred hours, had been shot down into the sea. He heard Joe shout, 'He must be saved!'

What he did not hear in the midst of all the parrot noise in his helmet was an order to ground-strafe the airfield. American Hellcats had done a good job on this already, however. They had destroyed a good bag of Jap machines on the ground and had slapped down one or two foolhardy enough to try and get off the runway. Some of 'Sam's' SBDs had bombed the field too, spare hands from the main dive-bombing attack on the oil storage tanks whom Jumping Joe had switched over when he saw that all the oil was burning in the sky.

On the whole the young Corsair pilots were so intent on their main job, so keen to carry it out to absolute perfection on this, their first operation, that after the Barracudas had dropped their bombs they overlooked many choice targets on the ground that more experienced opportunists would have strafed. But they did work over some ack-ack positions on the outskirts at the town and heavy ack-ack sites on a hill which lay in their path after they had pulled out of their first strafing dive.

And that was Sabang, come and gone. When they formed up and turned back on course, towards the ship they began to feel let down. The whole thing seemed unreal, too swift, gone in a flash. Concentrating feverishly on the difficulties of their own little individual jobs, they had been kept so preoccupied that all other impressions had escaped them. Only familiarity would bring awareness. Time alone would reveal to them the significance and full impact of all this violence.

Meanwhile, Sabang to them had been rather less exciting than a practice scramble from the ship. But if they did not realise what a success the strike had been, Jumping Joe came aboard *Illustrious* when they got back to Ceylon and put them right 'He seemed well satisfied,' was Norman's laconic entry.

Joe was particularly pleased because he had heard that his wingman was safe after all. Klahn had been rescued by the British submarine *Tactician* as the triumphant result of a piece of courage, coolness and seamanship which won the warmest admiration from the Americans. Commander Dose of '*Sara*' tells the story:

'One of our fighter pilots. Jumping Joe's wingman, was shot up by AA over the field, but managed to limp on – on fire – about three miles to sea where he baled out and manned his rubber life raft. I remained with twelve fighters, three divisions, to cover the downed pilot and the sub, while the groups departed and returned to the task force.

'The British submarine was stationed as rescue picket about fifteen miles north. The submarine, incidentally, had stayed on the surface during the entire attack watching the whole show.

'She proceeded immediately in the direction of the downed pilot. It took almost an hour to reach him. As the submarine approached a position about three miles from the pilot, his path took him fairly close and parallel to the shore line. At this point we observed large splashes within a submarine's length of the sub. The division of four which I had spotted above the airfield at 12,000 feet recognised the splashes as fire from a shore battery, spotted the battery, and strafed it into silence.

'The submarine, meanwhile, still surfaced, deviated not one degree from its course. It proceeded deliberately and calmly the remainder of the distance, picked up our pilot, and headed to sea and submerged.'

This was the sort of 'co-operation' both ships understood.

'We were much impressed,' says Commander Dose, 'with the courage and seamanship of the commander and crew of that submarine. They could have had anything we owned.'

CHAPTER EIGHT

THE PATTERN

'Life patterned in an unsure routine,' the Fleet Air Arm poet said. The
Illustrious pilots were used now to the sweat and discomfort of shipboard
routine, and they had done their first operation from the ship. Now, as the
next big job came up, they began to see another pattern taking shape – the
even more 'unsure' routine of operations.

Early in May *Illustrious*, with *Saratoga*, *Valiant*, *Renown*, the British cruiser
Gambia, French battleship *Richelieu* and Dutch cruiser *Tramp*, together with
a force of destroyers, went to Exmouth Gulf in Australia to refuel before
the next big strike. There wasn't much to see in this barren place –
'Burning sand. and sky atld nothing else,' noted Hanson.

This time it was to be Surabaya, in Java. Commander (Operations)
called the squadron commanders to the ready room.

The Captain has already told you that we and *Saratoga* are going to have
a crack at Japanese installations near Surabaya, on the north coast of Java.
This is how we're going to do it.

'*Saratoga*'s Dauntiesses are going to hit the oil refinery at Wonokromo,
which is six miles to the south of Surabaya. On the east side of this road is
the biggest engineering works in the Dutch East Indies – the Braat Works,
it's called. That's our target.

'Mike, your squadron will provide top cover for the bombing force. Hans, you will act as close escort – and here's where the sticky part comes in. We're going to be short of fighters, so your Corsairs are going to have to try to be in two places at once, or very nearly. First of all you will take the SBDs in to Wonokromo. As soon as you've seen them safely in you will go up the road and cover our Avengers making their run in on the Braat place. You should just about have time to do the two. You'd better go over to *Saratoga* and work out the details with Jim Hathorn. Now, let's have a look at the maps....'

When this conference was over Norman lost no time. Over on 'Sara' he found the dive-bomber skipper's cabin, knocked and stuck his head round the door.

'Wotcher, Jim!'

'Hello, Hans, what can I do for you?' said Hathorn. Lieutenant Commander Vincent L 'Jim' Hathorn, US Navy, was a regular Navy pilot with his job at his fingertips. His cabin shelves were jammed with books on dive-bombing technique, for dive-bombing was his hobby as well as his vocation.

'It's "what can I do for *you*?"' said Norman, grinning. 'I've been laid on to escort you.'

'Hell, and I thought I was going to come back from this one!' said Hathorn. 'Who talked you into it?'

'Churchill – he's giving me a bonus. How are we going to do it, Jim?'

'We'll,' began the American, brisk and serious at once, 'I want to start my dive at twelve thousand. I'll roll over on my back and the boys'll follow me down in sequence. We'll be doing between two-eighty, three hundred knots. When we've got going downhill I'd like you and your boys to go on ahead and shoot up anything in the way of flak you can see. It'll be bombs away at about four thousand. I'd like you to pick us up after we've reformed.'

'Well, you'll have to manage on your own for ten minutes, Jim, because after I've taken you down I've got to nip off with our chaps down to the Braat Works.'

'Hell, what about us?'

'Sorry, chum,' said Norman with a grin, 'we'll just have to do the best we can. Just head north into the bay and I'll pick you up when we come out. And for God's sake keep low on the water!'

'You bet your life,' said Hathorn grimly. 'Are you going to weave in flights or sections?'

'Oh, the usual good old American Thatch weave in sections. It might work.'

Hathorn grunted, grinning. Norman rose to go. The two were old friends by now, so there was no need for formalities.

'Look after yourself.'

'Okay. See you at the bull-fight.'

It was a tough assignment. The striking force would have ninety miles to go before they reached land – the coast of Java – then another hundred miles across the island to the target.

There was a sweat on in the hangar the night before, getting the aircraft ready. The great, oblong metal box beneath the flight deck was even more cramped for space than usual, for *Illustrious* had temporairily got rid of her Barracudas in exchange for bulky Grumman Avengers. These excellent American Navy bombers were very much better aircraft and they had the great advantage of being able to carry a heavier weight of bombs over a greater distance. Two squadrons of them were now in *Illustrious*, and they were very welcome.

There was no whooping it up for the aircrews that night. They spent the evening quietly and prepared for an early bed. Everyone, not only flying men, were very keyed up as they waited for action. Suddenly the loudspeakers blared.

'D'ye hear there! This is the Captain speaking. If anyone isn't too busy to come up on the flight deck there is something there worth seeing.'

They all scrambled up on deck expecting to see half the US Navy or the entire Japanese Fleet, or something of the sort. They stared about them for some minutes before they realised that the sea was completely empty – except for one of the most beautiful sunsets any of them had ever seen or were likely to see again.

Then it was straight to bed.

0100 hours. Haven't had a wink of sleep yet, just flying round the cabin doing bloody deck landings on the pillow.

'D'ye hear there! The Fleet will be going into action at 0700 hours this morning. Close up for action stations at 0600!'

Try to sleep once more, without much success.

Shaken at 0500. Dress, clumsy and, cursing – shift, flying overalls and gym shoes. Up to the wardroom where everybody toys with breakfast. (The stewards know better than to put anything decent on today.)

Back to the cabin to collect mae west and helmet. Up to the island and into the ready room to await the order. *Perhaps it won't come this morning. Perhaps the show's off.*

Suddenly the blowers roar:

'Pilots, man your aircraft!'

All the aircraft have been ranged the night before in order of take-off, fighters first, then bombers. Romp off down the flight deck and climb in. Two air merchants jump on to the wing and help to fix the straps. One of them says:

'Hit 'em, sir!'

Sit there, frightened as hell.

'Corsairs start up!' from Wings on the bridge.

Put the mag switch and fuel pump on. Put the booster pump on, hold it with one finger and press the starter with the other. Run the engine up with a roar to nine hundred revs and leave it there until everything is warmed through. The racket of sixteen Corsairs all doing the same is deafening.

'Avengers start up!'

The noise is so great that the order has to be relayed to the Avenger boys by the mechanics.

Then comes the worst moment of all.

Suddenly, there's the long, heavy noise of the aircraft liting up in front – the ship is turning into wind. You're for it now! It's a long way home and you can't get out and wait. *You shouldn't have joined!*

Everything begins to shudder as the ship works up to the twenty-seven knots necessary to get enough wind over the deck – the wind is a whisper in the Indian Ocean, and the ship has to make it all herself today.

The deck is spotted to the last inch, there is no room for mistakes. Musn't unlock the tail wheel too soon, or I might run into another prop.

Right. Out we go. Taxi into position for the take off, spread the wings and lock them properly as Johnny gives the signal, not forgetting to give him the thumbs up when you've done it. (That's a new rule brought in after poor old Monty bought it.) Lower flaps to maximum hard right rudder.

There's Bats 'winding me up' now. Open the engine to maximum and hold the brakes on.

A nod and Bats waves me up the deck.

Away you go laughing. Roar down the deck, past the bridge, up to the bows and off.

Once off the deck all one's worries cease. It's a beautiful morning and I'm flying and that's all there is to it.

Bank violently to starboard once clear of the deck and avoid flinging propwash back at the other aircraft behind.

The Wing Leader flies ahead of the ship for about a mile, pulls up his wheels and flaps and does a slow turn to port. Follow behind him downward out on the port side towards the joining up area astern of the ship.

Circle around there for a while, watching the others take off, then join up with the Americans.

And here we are, the whole strike. Hellcats, Corsairs, Dauntlesses. Avengers, the whole of our 'big blue team', roaring steadily through the bright sky together, wing and tail.

I look round and suddenly realise that life is a short thing, that I am lucky to have moments like this. *You'll be luckier still if you live to remember your beautiful thoughts.*

There's Jumping Joe out ahead of us all. And there's Rowbotham, leading the American Avengers. He's a descendent of Red Indian chiefs, as tough as ironwood, a great pilot.

'Strike leader to all aircraft. Setting course. Out.'

Everybody starts scrambling for height as fast as they can. It's a bloody uncomfortable job, climbing with the slow bombers, hanging on the prop at 130 knots, doing a very wide weave to keep down to their speed.

Okay, try and settle down now, enjoy the ride. We drone on over the glittering sea of Java.

There's the green of the coast now! How pretty it looks – real blue lagoon stuff.

God, it's *enemy* coast! All right, no more natter over the R/T. Keep your head on ball bearings from now on. Listen to the engine a bit more acutely too. There's only one – got to look after it.

Good Lord! Down below is a gently smoking, volcano!

Suddenly, with a shock – there's the sea! We're there!

Weave to and fro, looking into the faces of the bomber pilots – only a hundred feet away, some of them, and all going like dingbats now.

The signal from Bomber Leader. Go into echelon, with half the fighters on one side of the bombers, half on the other.

Watch Hathorn's SBD.

There he goes now – rolling over on his back. That means us.

Roll over and go down with him.

Down... down... down... pull out now... aah!

There's Jim Hathom pulling out.

Oh bloody good! He's put it slap bang into the middle of those cracker retorts!

The R/T crackles. Jim's voice –

'Don't waste your bombs, its finished.'

Okay, that's one lot. Now – up the road and see our chaps in.

There they are.

Now we're up with them. Down they go.

Oh lovely shooting! They're dropping them right through the letterbox with eleven and a half second fuses. Right on top of the engine works, not a single one on the road. There's a PoW camp on the other side of the road from the target. I bet the lads in there are getting a good view. A beautiful bit of bombing,

Now it's time to take the boys out to sea and pick up the Dauntlesses again. Down low over the water men, till it flashes past like a big steel plate. That's what it would feel like too if you ditched at this speed, so watch out for Nips.

Hello, look at that big bastard steaming in across the bay for Surabaya! Oh, we'll have to have a crack at you, chum! Down we go and give him a bellyful of armour piercing and incendiary.

Not bad shooting. I plastered the bridge good and proper, anyway.

Christ! Where did that lot come from!... It's tracer from the Hellcats beating up the harbour.

There's Jim and the SBDs. Good show.

Back home now with the bombers at 8,000 ft. Anybody missing? Seem to be one or two gaps. My lot's all right, anyway.

Here we are – back up the same valley and across the island. It's like being on rails. *Illustrious* here we come!

Bloody dull this – must be tired. Weaving, weaving, weaving, always bloody well weaving. Chrome pins and needles in the arse.

Hello! Who's that down there?

Four Hellcats... and four of our Corsairs.

What goes on? What the hell are they doing down there?

The R/T crackles. What was that?

Christ on a bicycle! It's an airfield! Must be Malang – we've come back up the *wrong* bloody valley! Oh well, not to worry, it's only Jap Army Air Corps HQ for Sumatra – that's all!

What are we waiting for! Let's go down and join the party! Wave the others down.

We've caught them with their pants down anyway, – that's something to be thankful for. There's not a gun manned down there, or an aircraft.

Woof! Right on a hangar! Good job you kept that bomb, chum – came in handy. Everybody having a go now. Avengers, Corsairs, – the lot. There's Bud Sutton and some of the 1830 boys having a go at the officers' mess. Rotten bastards! Breakfast time too!

Now it's our turn. They've got a few light guns pooping off now. Pay no regard. Look at that lovely line of parked aircraft! Here we go – give 'em both barrels! And another. There's a bod trying to get into a Myrtle. Oh good shot, Neil, that's fixed *him!*

Time to be going now. Head for home down the railway line. Dirty big black building down there. Some mean bastard giving it a squirt for luck with incendiaries. Jesus! The doors fly open and bodies pour out! Bad luck – right in the middle of the big picture! Roof on fire.

Okay, you've bad your fun. Join up with the main body and head back to the ship.

Surabaya was a great success. Mr Churchill sent a signal to the C-in-C, Eastern Fleet, Sir James Somervule, saying:

> 'I cordially congratulate you and your fleet and especially the aircraft crews upon the skilful execution and happy results of your operation of Surabaya. Please repeat my thanks to United States, French, and Dutch units which participated.'

Damage done was heavy and plane losses light. One of these, unfortunately, was Lieutenant Rowbotham, who ditched into the sea and was subsequently captured by the Japanese. It was learned after the war that he had been shot and killed by a Japanese guard.

Back in Ceylon Norman Hanson was sent for by Captain Cunliffe to explain why he had broken dose escort to strafe Malang. The Captain gave him a good dressing down. But he mentioned him in despatches afterwards, and recommended Mike Tritton, for a bar to his DSC.

Once again British and American pilots had worked splendidly together. But, as far as *Illustrious* and *Saratoga* were concerned, it was for the last time.

On completion of the Surabaya strike the combined fleet drew off to the southward. The following afternoon the *Saratoga* and her three destroyers parted company with their British, French and Dutch friends to return to the Pacific Fleet.

As they took leave of the Eastern Fleet a great demonstration was staged in their honour.

'"*Sara*" and her destroyers formed in column,' wrote Commander Dose. 'One by one past her port side steamed the entire array of Allied ships with which she had been associated for something over seven weeks. The column reached from horizon to horizon. As each man-of-war passed close abeam with such airs as "Auld Lang Syne" wafting across the interval and signal hoists spelling in the breeze their messages of goodwill, men and officers gave the traditional British "three cheers". We returned these honours in kind and in a Navy not given to cheering there were some raw throats that night.'

So departed '*Sara*', on a long cruise home which took her from the Indian Ocean to Puget Sound, and thence to Iwo Jima and the Kamikazes, to Tokyo and the end of the line.

She lies now on the bottom of Bikini Lagoon, sunk there in the atom bomb experiment of July, 1946. Surely no ship has rendered her country, and the whole free world, greater service than this great old lady.

As for Air Group 12, they were dispersed soon after '*Sara*' left the Indian Ocean, to spread their knowledge and skill among the new airmen about to join the Fleet.

In their fifteen months of hard fighting from Pearl Harbour to Surabya they had put up a score which few units have ever equalled. In all that time they lost only twelve of their own planes to enemy action, with three men killed and twenty missing. They destroyed a hundred and two enemy planes, sank 104,500 tons of shipping and damaged another 198,500 tons.

It was a splendid record and representative of the great things the US Navy had done and continued to do in the Far East

It left *Illustrious* with an example – and a challenge.

But they felt confident and ready for anything now. Actor Robert Eddison, who shared a cabin with Bob Ellison, remarked after Surabaya in his rather prim manner,

'I've wasted a very great deal at emotion on that operation. I shall never do such a thing again.'

The doctor rather agreed with him. In tact it was, roughly speaking, what the whole ship felt. They had been blooded, they were in the swing of action, and they felt ready to settle down a little more to the routine of work and play which would, fill their days for some time to come.

The ship was fortunate in having a number of ex-actors on board at this time, all of whom were doubly useful in being able to entertain as well as carry out their normal executive duties. Besides Eddison, there was Michael Hordern, who was the ship's Fighter Direction Officer, Douglas Storm, and Malcolm Baker-Smith, too, who was a writer and another exile from the far off world of show business. Between them these men put on many a successful show which helped morale enormously.

When there were no aircraft airborne, and nothing on the radar screen, the theatrical expatriates would often produce mugs of tea and gather in Ellison's cabin to talk theatre. They were in full spate one day when the Captain put his head round the door, gasped at the flow of theatrical jargon, and said,

'What the hell is this? A meeting of ENSA?'

But there were no meetings of ENSA when the time came for the next op.

The squadrons were busy as soon as the ship returned from Surabaya. There were R/T and interception exercises, section flying, height climbs and fighter direction exercises. Twice Norman Hanson flew to Coimbatore to collect new aircraft and, flight test them.

On July 11th the Corsairs did a beat-up of the cruiser *Phoebe*. On the 13th and 15th Hordern and his colleagues were kept busy controlling the Corsairs in more fighter direction exercises.

The busy CO of 1833 was so occupied that he started to get behindhand with his diary. On the 14th he found time to scribble:

'...Oh! I forgot! Given a copy of this today – "Your 060725. 'Concur in Lt. (A) Hanson commanding 1833

Squadron. He is granted acting rank of Lt.-Cdr. (A) from 20th March, 1944".'

On the 16th they did an escort and attack practice on China Bay. The practice, however, was more for the attackers than for the defences, for their next strike was only five days away.

This time it was Port Blair in the South Andaman Islands, and the Barracudas had been brought back to do the job. Port Blair, an old penal settlement, was another important Japanese staging point for their forces in Burma and its destruction would help to take the pressure off our troops fighting on that desperate 'forgotten' front.

Norman was detailed off to lead a strafing force on this tempting target. 1833 was not, at this stage, a ground strafing squadron, but some of 1830 had had experience of it. Norman talked over the situation with Mike Tritton.

'Take Percy Cole's lads with you,' said Mike, who as senior fighter commander had been made Fighter Wing Leader after Dickie Cork's death, 'they're good ground strafers.'

So the two squadrons swapped pilots. It was arranged that Norman should take his own flight and that of Pery Cole. Cole was a skilled ground strafer and a most polished pilot altogether, a man whose landings all the younger pilots were always told to watch for points. The idea was for Norman's eight Corsairs to go in at low level before the bombers had left the ship to clear the way for them.

There was nothing unusual about this bit of squadron barter; it happened all the time now. The Wing, in fact, really *was* a wing, no mere arbitrary combination of two squadrons, and Mike led it with tact and coolness. It was a team, with everybody joining forces in friendly co-operation.

This feeling began with the squadron ratings. Men from both circuses would readily lend a hand with advice and technical help in a hearty 'One, two, six – *heavy*!' across the hangar deck.

Many of the pilots started off with the advantage of having known one another from training days. It soon became a common thing for one pilot to offer to do another's 'stand by on deck' or 'readiness'. Mike and Norman, too, who had adjoining cabins, had become increasingly friendly. The two COs would often share serviceable aircraft and eventually, when they had sized up their pilots, they began to exchange flights for specialist jobs, such as the present operation on Port Blair. Sometimes even a flight of four contained men from both squadrons.

It was a filthy morning when the mixed force took off. They had to fly a hundred miles through low cloud and rain and hit a target that was known to be bristling with light flak.

They flew six feet from the wave tops all the way, to dodge enemy radar. By the time they approached the South Andaman coast they had exhausted all the fuel in their auxiliary wing tanks. Empty, but full of inflamable petrol vapour, these tanks had to be purged by the injection of carbon dioxide from bottles in the cockpit. As they caught sight of their check point. North Sentinel Island, away to starboard, Norman gave the order to purge wing tanks. They all complied without mishap – except Gordon Aitken, who found the wrong lever and operated the emergency bottle which blew his undercarriage down. It was a very easy thing to do, as the two controls were side by side, but it left Gordon with a fixed undercarriage. Corsair wheels, once locked down by the emergency device, could not be unlocked short of an engineering job. With its trousers round its ankles, his Corsair a complete liability and Norman sent him packing back to the ship.

After North Sentinel Island, South Andaman lay dead ahead. Coming in over the sea from the west, they made for the head-land which was their next check point, turned there ninety degrees to starboard and roared in overland towards Port Blair, which lay on the coast on the far side of the South Andaman island-promontory, circling round again to port so as to come in to the target on a course of 102 degrees, and out again an a reciprocal course of 286. For anyone hit over the target area a rescue submarine waited in a position halfway between South Andaman and North Sentinel.

They split into the two flights so as to attack from opposite sides. The airfield lay to the south side of the town – two strips hacked out of the jungle, with a dim line of aircraft parked at the north end of it.

Percy Cole immediately led his flight off to make their approach from the south side of the field, while Norman's lads climbed up into the murky rain to the north and strained their eyes through the gloom trying to make out details of the planes below.

Then Cole gave the word and started his run in. As his Corsair roared down the middle of the airstrip, leading the attack, the whole airfield burst into flame. Guns lining both sides of the strip flung out a wild hurricane of fire. Cole and his Corsairs ran the gauntlet of them, their own guns answering back as they raked the field and the parked planes at the far end. The Japaneses aircraft, hit in their unprotected tanks, started to explode in flames.

Norman saw Cole's plane down low against the greenery, heard his crisp 'All clear!' and took his own flight down for their run in.

White faces looked up as the Corsairs appeared out of the rain. Tiny figures tried to out-run three hundred knots as the 'Whistling Death' howled in on them. The Corsairs held their fire until lethal range, then gloved fingers on firing buttons released a torrent of yammering .5 that tore into the planes which Cole's flight had left, setting them off like great fireworks among the fiercely burning bonfires of 1830's victims, while Reggie Shaw raced down the side of the field, knocking petrol bowsers and airfield installations into blazing wreckage.

There was a trench crammed with tight ack-ack across the bottom of the field. The gunners there did not duck or run away. As Hans flung his machine headlong at them he could see his bullets hitting the ground all around the Japanese as they stood without flinching and shook the Corsair with bursting shells.

Now they could hear the planes of the main strike over the R/T. Cole stayed over the airfield while the 1833 boys made for the radar station on Mount Harriet, to the north of the harbour.

The radar station was three long, low huts with a flimsy wooden lattice-work tower carrying the aerials. They beat it up with armour-piercing and incendiary, watching their bullets striking the ribs of the mast and the aerials.

'Watch that bastard with the machine-gun up on the mast!' said Norman. A few seconds later -

'Okay, boss, I got him,' came the crackle from Regie Shaw.

Suddenly it was over, and they were jogging along together over jungle and mangrove at two hundred feet on their way back to *Illustrious*. Norman thought: 'What a helluva place to ditch.

'Hey, boss,' came Neil Brynildsen's Kiwi tones in his ears, 'we're a bit too high – they're firing at us down there!'

At that precise second Norman's plane was hit.

He felt the Corsair shudder and rear up and saw bits of metal tear off like lettuce leaves from the cowling.

Down went the flight to zero altitude, then away at full throttle for the safety of the sea.... *God! I nearly had it!*

When he got back to the ship he found that shell fragments had knocked the vanes off number one cylinder and left rosettes of curling metal where they had come out of the cowling. But he had got back safely and so had all the other Corsairs. Johnny Baker's plane had been hit in the radio compartment and had taken a cannon shell through the propeller blade. One bomber had been lost when it crashed into Port Blair harbour.

It looked as if the Japs were getting rougher. However, losses were light this time and those who had got back with a few dents were thankful for small mercies.

> 'I congratulate you and all concerned,' said C-in-C Eastern Fleet in a signal to Rear-Admiral Moody, 'especially the aircraft crews on the very successful outcome of the operation....'

On that note they felt they could relax a little – until the next lot. When they got back to Trincomalee the fly-boys let their hair down.

While they were in this time their new Captain came on board.

The buzz found something highly significant in this, and in the fact that Their Lordships' choice was Captain Charles Lambe, one of the most brilliant young captains on the Navy List.

On July 8th the Corsairs showed him what they could do. 'A day at sea today with the new Captain,' Norman writes, 'flew twice on exercises – not bad. No prangs, anyway, thank God! And no blacks!'

Then on July 9th he makes the sad entry:

> 'We pulled our old Captain, God bless him, ashore in a cutter today. He was given a wonderful send-off by the ship's company – clinging to rivets on the port side, in order to see him leave by the port after gangway. We shall miss him very much.'

Captain Cunliffe had indeed been loved and respected by all aboard. One thing the aircrews loved about him was his constant concern for their safety and well-being. Once, when Bob Ellison was watching a land-on from the bridge, a Barracuda dived headlong into the sea, taking its crew with it. At that instant Ellison happened to glance at the Captain's face – and saw it age ten years.

Pilots felt that perhaps a little beer and skittles *was* in order now. On July 15th, 1833 celebrated an event in its history, which was recorded by 'Schoolie' Jenkins, and found its way into the Line Book:

'July 15th, 1943, at Quonset Point, Rhode Island, was formed the third British Corsair Squadron... 1833.'

In August it moved to Brunswick, Maine, for further training. Eventually it crossed to England in HMS *Trumpeter* and joined HMS *Illustrious* in the Clyde.

'Since its inception, the Squadron has flown 2,700 hours and done 460 deck landings, whilst altogether it has downed fifty-one aircraft.

They are now as much a part of us as our chimney, and I know tfaat I speak tor all when I say "Many Happy Returns".

'Today is also St Swithin's Day.... According to the old, old story, if it rains today it will rain on the next forty days and nights, but the Met Officer says it is all!'

The happy occasion nevertheless turned into a wet one. Norman also took the opportunity of expressing the pilots 'appreciation of twelve months' hard and faithful support from the squadron ratings.

'The officers join me,' he said, 'in thanking you sincerely for – your congratulations and good wishes on this our first birthday.

Let us hope mat the coming year will see our good fortune and success smiling on us.

'To all of you we wish to say a very sincere "Thank you" for your loyalty end untiring devotion to duty during our first year.

We all understand how difficult it can be out here; prickly heat, long hours of "overtime" in the hangar and the eternal heat *all* do their best to pull a man down to his lowest.

'But stick at it... it can't last for ever, and if we weren't doing *this* we should probably be doing something the *hell* of a lot worse!

'So – work hard, whatever you do, do it conscientiously, try to be as cheerful as possible; and Good Luck to all of you.'

The buzz about leave was true, but the 'scions of the sea' had one more op to do first. 'The lure of distant lands,' said Steve Starkey's Line Book, 'takes us back to Sabang.'

They had done Port Blair alone, and it had been quite enough for one air group to cope with. Now, five days before the second smack at Sabang, they got reioforcemems. *Victorious* arrived in Trincomalee. 'High bloody time too!' wrote the hard-working CO of 1833.

'Thirty-eight Corsairs deck landing today – and only one burst tyre.... 'Quite a succeful day!'

Victorious was coming with them to Sabang, bringing her own Corsairs to swell the attack. For this was to be practically an all-fighter show, in support of a bombardment by the guns of the Fleet.

One Corsair section of two aircraft was to spot for the big guns of each of the capital ships – battleships *Queen Elisabeth*, *Valiant*, *Richelieu* and the battle-cruiser *Renown*. The battle-wagons were being supported by the fire of six cruisers, *Gambia*, *Nigeria*, *Cumberland*, *Kenya*, *Ceylon* and *Tramp*, and there was a force of ten destroyers, whose main role was to carry out a cutting-out dash into the harbour and attack with torpedoes.

The eight Corsairs spotting for the big guns were to have another twelve fighters to protect them, while the remainder of the air striking force was divided into two parts, an *Illustrious* force to strike Sabang itself, and the other, a mixed *Victorious/Illustrious* group, to strike the airfield at Koetaradja, close by on the mainland of Sumatra.

Some of *Victorious'* Corsairs were switched to the other carrier for the operation to assist the exact arrangement of numbers for the different roles which the fighter force were to have to play. Norman Hanson took ten Corsairs for the Sabang strike – his own flight, Bud Stutton's from 1830 and a section of 1837 Squadron from *Victorious*, their main targets the airfield and radar installations.

In all, *Illustrious* put up forty-two Corsairs and nine Barracudas, *Victorious* thirty-eight Corsairs. Eighty fighters ought to be able to do some damage.

They did, and so did the big guns of the Fleet. It was a satisfactory strike from all points of view. Norman, in his official 'Report on Strafing Operations at Sabang: July 25th, 1944', tells the story thus:

> 'We took off from *Illustrious* in poor light at 0535, and were joined up in formation at 0545. Proceeded at 180 knots, and made a good landfall on the west coast of Sabang Island at 0558....
>
> The light was so bad that visibility over the airfield was almost too poor for strafing, and we found it almost impossible to recognise objects on the ground....'

On the first run in they nevertheless destroyed aircraft on the ground, barrack blocks and radar installations.

> 'On the second run over the target area, fire was concentrated on the hangars, machine-gun posts, and the easterly mast of the radar installation.'

They made three more sweeps of the whole target area, setting buildings on fire and shooting-up gun positions.

> 'I made my run over the town,' continued Hanson, 'and continued over the

airfield to press home our attack on the heavy AA battery on the south side of the airfield. I opened on the battery from about 1,000 yards, and, as I closed, concentrated on one gun, the crew of which I feel pretty sure I killed.'

The ack-ack was very intense and damaged three of the Corsairs. By now the battlewagons were shooting. The earth shook as 15-inch shells screamed in from the ships eight miles away, the great blast waves made the ground ripple like water. Norman saw an entire building rise in one piece, then fall again to the ground. Then it was time to work over the harbour. The report continues:

'We attacked a heavily laden merchant ship, estimated about 5,000 tons, from astern, and my No. 4 saw fire breaking out in the after part as he passed over it. We swept over the harbour and machine-gunned warehouses on the wharves and quays....'

They finally landed-on again aboard *Illustrious* at 0730, conscious of a job well done. The heavy guns of the Fleet had done a workmanlike job too and heavy damage had been caused.

Our men in Burma were not as 'forgotten' as they imagined.

Casualties had been light. One of the spotter escorts from 1830 was hit and set on fire, the pilot being hit and his left arm paralysed by splinters. But he baled out-one-handed over Sabang town and was blown out to sea by the strong wind. Shore batteries fired at him as he floated, but the cruiser *Nigeria* came up, silenced the battery, and picked up the pilot.

'I consider this. has been a very good party,' signalled the C-in-C, 'in that all units taking part acquitted themselves most creditably, I am sure everyone will pin the in congratulating the Inshore Force on their spirited close action....

'It was nice work, pretty to see and better still to have – taken part in.'

'And so,' said the Line Book, 'back to Trinco, where officers of His Majesty's Forces can get away from these wars, but not away from the whisky shortage.'

Then they put out and headed – west, this time, for rest and refreshment, with Cape Town first stop.

CHAPTER NINE

THE THIRTY YEARS WAR

It was strictly 'business with pleasure', the business a boiler refit at Durban for *Illustrious*, the pleasure, long delayed, an uninhibited holiday for two thousand leave-happy sailors.

But the squadrons had to wait a day or two for theirs. The airfield at Durban being too small to take them, the ship went down to Cape Town and launched planes there. A nod and a wink would have been quite enough for some of the more light-headed to have deck landed on Table Mountain, but encouragement was not forthcoming and they all put down at Wingfield Aerodrome. The ship came in to unload squadron ratings and stores, and after a rousing weekend left for Durban and her refit. Three days after moving in to Wingfield, the air squadrons went on leave, the ratings for two weeks, the aircrews for three. They disappeared into Cape Town and various other parts of sunny South Africa, and for a short while everything was quiet.

Then those left with the ship at Durban began to receive wild rumours of riot. *Illustrious'* repressed airmen, it seemed, were taking the place apart. Nights were lurid, days were spent in bed charging batteries for the orgy of painting Cape Town red, white and blue. 'Blonde Blitz!' announced the Line Book in later days of wistful recollection, 'A pleasure That Has Never

Changed!'

Every day brought in fresh wild stories. Barracudas were reported crashing all over Table Mountain, and somebody was supposed to be facing court martial for beating up the private residence of the Commander-in-Chief of the South African Army.

The squadrons seemed to be disintegrating so rapidly that Bob Ellison was despatched hastily to Cape Town. When he arrived at Wingfield, he found that one, at least, of the rumours was true, in the shape of a disconsolate Norman Hanson sitting alone in the mess – grounded and under open arrest. It was a sad story he had to tell.

He had gone on leave with Fanny Forde. In the course of their pleasure they had met a crowd of genial and hospitable Springboks. One of them, Nick Loew, had entertained Norman at his country place, a huge estate where he went in for wine production from his own wine farm and wine presses, and bred horses. Nick was fanatically keen on aeroplanes, but 'Retreat' was thirty miles from Cape Town and he hardly ever even saw one.

'Why don't you fly over here sometimes?' he asked Norman.

'I'd like to have a look at one of those Corsairs of yours.'

Norman remembered this a few days later. It was getting near embarkation time now. Most of the squadron had gone ashore and he was up doing an air test on his Corsair, which had just had a new magneto fitted.

He was looking down idly at the countryside when he recognised Nick Loew's place. Going lower, he picked out Nick's bathing pool – and there was Nick himself standing by the side of the pool, waving. Norman remembered his request and put the nose of the Corsair down in a screaming dive to give Nick something to remember.

He flattened out at zero feet about two miles, away from 'Retreat' and came whistling in towards it on the deck, hedge-hopping between the trees. He did half a dozen of these strafing runs on the pool, then, with a wave at Nick, went up to seven thousand feet and went through a complete routine of aerobatics before he turned and made for Wingfield.

He flew back gaily, the only pilot in the air, and put his Corsair down with a flourish. Whistling happily and swinging his helmet in his hand, he swept into the squadron office.

'*Good* morning, sir!' he said to John Smallwood, their new Air Operations Officer.

'Good morning,' said Smallwood a trifle less cordially. 'Nice up this morning?'

'Oh, absolutely bang on, sir, glorious!' said the happy warrior.

'How many Corsairs up?'

'Oh, just me, sir, just me!'

'I see. Have you been low flying in Cape Town?'

'low fly... *No*, sir!'

'Where *have* you been?'

'Oh, just round and about, sir, just round and about.'

H'm. Look at this map,' said Smallwood grimly. He looked. It was a large map of the Cape Town area and there was a huge blue ring round Nick Loew's estate. Smallwood pointed to the letters A6A scribbled in the margin,

Is that you?'

'Yes, sir.'

'Who lives at this place?'

'Friend of mine named Nick Loew, sir,'

'Been there this morning?'

'Yes.'

'You've been low flying, haven't you?'

'Well... that's a matter of opinion.'

'Well, *how* low *were* you?'

'Oh, you know how it is... anywhere from about six hundred feet down...'

'Yes, well, it's *my* opinion that it was more like *six* feet!'

'Oh, that's ridiculous, sir!' (*Six feet – thats an insult to a ground strafing squadron. It was less than that.*)

'Anyway, have you any idea who lives next door to your friend?'

'No, sir.'

'Only the General Officer commanding all troops in South Africa! He's put in a complaint and the Admiral is determined to make an example of you. You'll have to see the Captain.'

A very chastened Norman saw the CO of Wingfield, Captain Farquahar, the same man who had been Captain at St Merryn when Norman was there.

'I've done what I can for you, Hanson,' he said, 'but the Admiral is adamant. I'm afraid it means a court martial.'

So he was grounded and put under open arrest, pending court-martial proceedings. Miserably he continued to drink alone in the mess, brooding over the thought of his impending disgrace. One night Captain Farquahar came in and joined him.

'You know, this is a bad business,' he said sympathetically. 'What does Captain Lambe think about it?'

'Oh, he'll play hell when he hears about it, sir.'

'What!' said the Captain. 'Do you mean to say you haven't *told* him?'

In a matter of minutes he had got in touch with the Captain of *Illustrious* by tele-printer.

Rushing back into the mess, he said, "He's given me a new line of action' – and showed Norman the last line of a reply from Captain Lambe, which read: 'Above all, Hans must not worry about this. Everything will be all right.'

The 'new line of action' worked quickly. Next day Norman was brought before the C.-in-C., Admiral Burnett, and, after the most terrible dressing-down he had ever had in his life, was let off with a caution.

The magic formula had been a call by Captain Farquahar upon the General himself, who, horrified when he was told that the offender stood to lose his squadron, his half-ring and be sent home in disgrace, refused to appear at the court martial and press charges.

Norman, of course, went straight out to call on the General personally and apologise.

The old soldier, General I P de Villiers, had once fought against us in a Boer commando. With a twinkle in his eye be poured the young pilot a drink.

'I didn't want them to go to all those lengths, my boy,' he said, 'but, you see, what happened was this. I had got up a bit latish that morning, after a party the night before. I was in the bathroom looking out of the window and thinking how beautiful the Mountain looked that morning, when... Whoosh!... an aeroplane came roaring over my lawn, *underneath* my window. I was just wondering what had happened when... Whoosh! ... it happened again. You were so low that I could read your identification letters! It was very dangerous, my boy – you might have killed yourself. Very silly, very silly! Then, afterwards, you went up where you should have been in the first place and did some very nice stunt flying. What was that one where you go up in a loop and then...'

Norman was never so relieved before. Thanks to the team spirit of *Illustrious* he was saved. He went back thankfully to a programme of attacks, air tests, flight tactics and escort practice nights at Wingfield. The programme was an intensive one, and besides the normal items of fighter work, particular emphasis was being laid on ground strafing, and upon a new item – dive-bombing. It looked as if something big was in the wind.

The practice was doubly needed, as there had been some changes in the squadrons. In 1833, New Zealanders Neil Brynildsen, Matt Barbour and Ken Seebeck had gone home on leave and mere had been an influx of new faces. Said the Line Book:

'At Wingfield occurred following short story:

$$1833 + \frac{1838}{2} = 1833'$$

The new contingent, all ex-1838 Squadron, was strongly Dominion in character. 'Winnie' Churchill, Jack Parli, Ben Heffer and Evan Baxter all came from New Zealand, and Jerry Morgan from Canada.

Most of them were gay, happy-go-lucky types, especially the wild combination of Churchill and Parli. Winnie was an enormous personality, a young bull roaring with energy, a tough, fearless pilot who had been at Salerno and knew a trick or two – both in the air and on deck, where he and Parli kept many a party going by their side-splitting impression of an all-in wrestling match. Jimmy James was a light-hearted product of Dartmouth, a good pilot and an entertaining companion.

These additions built the squadron up to twenty men and eighteen machines. This was too large for one senior pilot to maintain, so it was divided into two units, with Bash Munnoch and Jack Parli as Senior Pilots, each in charge of one team.

The squadrons rejoined *Illustrious* from Wingfield on October 13th and the Corsairs aviated constantly, with visual and radar fighter direction exercises, escort practices and mock attacks on the ship filling their days.

On the last day of October, with *Illustrious* at sea heading east again for Ceylon, the following announcement appeared in the *London Gazette*:

'ADMIRALTY
Whitehall, 31st October. 1944

The KING has been graciously pleased to approve
the following rewards and awards:

For outstanding courage, skill and determination in
pressing home a successful attack on the Japanese
Naval base at Sabang:'

There followed a long list of officers, petty officers and ratings who had been honoured. Among the awards of the Distinguished Service Cross were:

'Temporary Lieutenant-Commander (A) ,
Norman Stanley Hanson, RNVR (Carlisle)

Temporary Lieutenant (A) Percival Sidney Cole,
RNVR (Potters Bar, Middlesex)'

It was one apiece for 1830 and 1833. Another pilot had also been awarded a DSC, and others from *Illustrious* had been mentioned in despatches, including Rear-Admiral Moody himself, and pilots Bud Sutton of 1830 and Alan Booth of 1833.

Norman did not hear of his award until November 3rd. His diary records simply: 'Met Wings, who tells me I have been awarded a DSC! Whoopee!!'

Just after they left South Africa the Barracudas flew ashore. 'Barracudas left the deck for the last time,' said the Line Book, 'and we returned to the jungle.' They were not sorry to see the last of these odd flying fish. Starkey posted a clipping in the Line Book which quoted 'the insignificance of the barracuda, a fish which has been getting a big build-up in the penny dreadfuls in the last few years,' Fanny Forde and his boys, however, were a great loss to the ship.

Soon they were back among the fickle winds of the Indian Ocean. Just before they put into Trincomalee, Wings, sent for the two Corsair COs.

'It looks,' said 'Sarel, 'as it we're going to be in harbour for a week or two, and I'd like some aircraft to go ashore to keep the chaps' hands in. How many are you going to take?'

Norman looked at Mike Tritton. 'I'd thought of taking eight, Mike. How about you?'

'Yes, I think eight's about ample for all I want. I'm mainly interested, in doing ADDL's with my new boys.'

'Are you going to try and work in some air-to-air firing?' said Sarel.

'Yes,' said Mike, I think we'd better try and take some drogues ashore.'

'We might as well get in some air-to-ground, too, while we're at it,' put in Norman.

'Right,' said Wings, 'I'll make a signal and let them know what we want.'

First, the Corsairs flew off to Kogalla airfield in south-western Ceylon. Kogalla was a single strip with one end on the sea and the other on, a lagoon. All resemblance to a tropical paradise ended there, however. The field was surrounded by jungle and abounded with wild life of all unpleasant descriptions – lizards, salamanders, cobras, Russell's vipers, fireflies and mosquitoes – and everyone carried revolvers and heavy sticks for protection. It was so hot at Kogalla that every afternoon was a make-and-mend and everyone got their heads down and dozed out of the sun, or swam lazily in the blue water.

They left their blue lagoon on November 26th and moved to China Bay, but not before they had lost one of the new pilots, Canadian Jerry Morgan, who spun into the sea.

At China Bay they stepped up their programme, ADDL's, escorts and strikes were increased. *Indomitable*, her old stable-mate, now joined

Illustrious.

It looked like a build-up for something big, and the signs did not lie. A few weeks earlier Churchill and Roosevelt had met in Quebec, and there it had been agreed that the Royal Navy should participate in the final onslaught on Japan. Roosevelt made one important condition. The British Fleet in the Pacific must be self-supporting. This would raise serious problems for the Navy, as they would have no base nearer the forward area than Australia. But the Navy had solved worse problems before, and in any case it was high time a British Battle Fleet appeared in Australian waters, where American senior officers had commanded all Allied forces seen there hitherto. Britain also wanted a strong vote in the post-war settlement of the Far East, where British interests before the war had been far greater than American.

It was now decided, therefore, to divide the old Eastern Fleet into a Pacific Fleet and an East Indies Fleet. Admiral Sir Bruce Fraser would command the British Pacific Fleet, which would comprise all our newest and fastest ships, and would work with the US Pacific Fleet under Fleet-Admiral Nimitz as soon as arrangements could be made for its supply. Admiral Power, formerly the Vice-Admiral Second in Command of the Eastern Fleet, was to take over command of the East Indies Fleet, which would consist of some old battleships and a force of escort carriers, cruisers, destroyers and submarines, and would continue to support our campaign in Burma and the operations in Malaya planned for a later stage.

The training went on, with Norman particularly concerned about ground strafing. He hadn't forgotten those ack-ack guns along the airstrip at Port Blair and at Sabang. They had been lucky to get away with some of those beat-ups. Now was the time to try to correct some of their mistakes – before it was too late and the next strike was upon them.

'Steve,' he told the hard-worked adjutant, 'arrange for all pilots to be up in the squadron office at nine, will you? I want to talk to them.'

'Now look,' he said, when they were all together. 'On our last op the last run-in on that airfield was very ragged – some of us are damn lucky to be here to talk about it. If we've got to do that sort of thing again we must do our run-in across the airfield exactly abreast, no matter which way we come in to attack, otherwise the chap lagging astern is going to get all the stuff that was meant for me. We've already decided that if the airfield is a one-strip job, they automatically expect us to run the whole length down it – we learned that one on the Andaman show – and they'll be waiting for us to do it again. The only successful way of doing it is to approach one end of the runway at right-angles when we're going downhill pretty fast and then do a rapid ninety-degree turn to port on to the line of the airstrip.'

'Boss' – one of the lads stuck up his hand.

'Yes?'

'I think the flight leader, when we're going downhill, should be in the right-hand section. The lads who have to slide under will have a lot more room if they're moving to the outside rather – than to the inside of the turn.'

'Yes, that's a jolly good point. You might remember that, chaps. If you're not in that position when you run downhill, *get* yourself into it. Look, I'll give you a rough idea of what I mean on the blackboard. Here's the airfield, here's our line of approach. Round about *here* we should be going downhill at a good rate of knots – certainly no less than three hundred – and this is where we should go into our ninety-degree turn. I'm hoping that the approach will be long enough to enable everybody to get into line abreast and *not* long enough to let the Japs get one in on us!'

'Why don't we get upstairs and have a crack at it?' said one eager voice.

'I don't see why we should stooge around in the air just because we have clots in our midst!' chipped in another.

'Ha! Look who's talking...'

'Anyway, that's what we're going to do in half an hour's time,' said Norman and turned to Starkey. 'Steve, ring up Minneriyah and ask if they'd mind us doing a practice run across the airfield.'

That was the usual form. A little later would see them all up over the Jungle strip, putting blackboard theory into practice:

'Open the taps a bit, Johnny.'

'Okay, Skipper – got a bit lost on the turn.'

Then, towards the end of their trip ashore, one of the batsmen, Colin Cunningham or Johnny Hastings, would come ashore to lead them through some final ADDL's before rejoining the ship.

On December 1st a squadron of twenty Avengers landed aboard under the command of Charlie Mainprice, and were immediately made welcome. The buzz at once quickened with the deduction that the next show must be a long-range effort. On December 3rd there was a bad carrier crash, and on the 7th, Matt Barbour celebrated his return from leave by putting his Corsair over on ils back on me flight deck.

'Must have been a bloody good leave,' said someone. Matt was lucky to get out alive from the wreckage.

With him from New Zealand came Jimmy Clarke, who had been Norman's number two on the last Sabang show. Now that they knew Neil Brynildsen had gone to *Victorious* he got the job permanently. Ken Seebeck was another old 1833 boy who never landed on *Illustrious* again. In fact he never made another deck landing, for as soon as he returned from leave he was posted to the UK to learn a batsman's job.

Things moved fast now. On December 8th the *Illustrious*'s Corsairs made an attack on *Indomitable*, '*Indom*'s Hellcats shot us all down,' wrote Norman mournfully in his diary. On the 9th another carrier, *Indefatigable*, arrived to join the rapidly increasing task force. The main strength of a great battle fleet now lay swinging round the buoy in Trincomalee.

December 14th was a day to note. It was the day Vian came.

The new Rear-Admiral, Aircraft Carriers, flew on board in an Avenger in the afternoon, and the ship's Corsairs put on a show for him, with a practice strike on the ship. That afternoon Vian came into the wardroom and spoke to all the officers of the air squadrons.

Of course, they all knew his history. But as he stood there and spoke to them it was easy to guess, even if you didn't knows that this was a man who would handle destroyers like a fighter his fists, and a carrier fleet like a commando platoon. This was Vian of the *Cossack*.

He stood there, foursquare and uncompromising, stiff and unsmiling, with a brown, lined seaman's face, and gave them the benefit of his blunt wisdom.

He did not know, he said, what their individual experience of action might have been, but they could be certain, when they got around into the Pacific – which was where they were all going – that they would all get a lot more action than they had ever seen before. When a ship was in action all the time, it was vital that morale should be preserved from the highest level down. They, perhaps, had never been in a ship when she was being knocked about. It was then that it was most essential to keep morale high. When a ship was hit – especially by a six – or fifteen-inch shell or a bomb – they might see bits of arms and legs and other remains lying about. If they did – on this ship – they must not pause and think sad thoughts, but immediately fling the pieces overboard. To leave them about would certainly be bad for morale, would start men thinking when they should be fighting.

Then he flew back to *Indomitable,* which wore his flag.

On December 15th the battleship *King George V* arrived. Now the heart of a great new fleet was here at Trincomalee – carriers, battleships, cruisers and destroyers swinging at anchor together. It was the British Pacific Fleet, and its target was Tokyo. Soon these fine ships, as proud a sight as a British admiral had ever seen from his flag bridge, would head east and into the ocean battleground of the Rising Sun. They were Admiral Fraser's ships, and his second-in-command's, Vice-Admiral Power, who would lead them at sea.

But the carriers, and their men, were Vian's – Vian's in body, Vian's in heart and soul. He and his flat-tops were the heart of the BPF, and when his Corsairs and Hellcats, Seafires and Avengers flew, it was he who assumed tactical control of the Fleet. This was American practice and new to the Royal Navy, but it fitted that fierce, hard man to have this power, for he was our Halsey, picked because in battle he knew nothing else but to fight.

The fight was soon on. On the 20th *Illustrious* and *Indomitable* put out to strike Belawan Deli, in Sumatra.

The task force headed east across the familiar blue plains of the Indian Ocean. Ahead, below the horizon, stretched the great convex of islands, the vast outer barrier of Japanese dominion stretching from Rangoon in the north, south through the Andamans and the Sunda necklace – Sumatra, Java,,Bali, Lombok, Flores and the rest – through Timor to New Guinea. Previously, British carriers operating from Ceylon had struck and paralysed centres of supply skin-deep inside this shield – Sabang, Surabaya, Port Blair. But they had always done so from outside, the Indian Ocean side, and their planes had had to fly overland before they found their targets.

But this time mey did not stop outside. They went inside the barrier. Right past Sabang they steamed and round into Japanese waters, to close their target – Pangkalan Brandan, another big oil refinery and staging point for Burma, lying across the Malacca Straits from Penang, in the southern Malay peninsula. Now the striking force could attack from seaward with no long flight overland to give the Japs ample warning. Of course, the Fleet was sticking its neck out. In fact, it was strongly suspected among the pilots that Vian would have enjoyed enticing heavy Japanese units up from Singapore and giving his planes a chance at them.

The planes of the Pangkalan strike left the two carriers' decks – in uncertain weather. Once airborne, they had to climb above an overcast so thick as to obscure completely the entire view below from horizon to horizon. With no means of taking a fix, the strike leader's aircraft was forced to navigate by dead reckoning.

Eventually the striking force reached a position approximately over the target area and the strike leader led the whole group down through the overcast – nearly sixty aircraft, Avengers, Corsairs and Hellcats.

Visibility was appalling. They saw coastline but could not recognise anything that looked like Pangkalan Brandan. So once again the whole force climbed up into the overcast at low speed. As they did so they exposed themselves dangerously to whatever Japanese fighters might be up from the big airfield of Medan, nearby. But they were lucky – the murk lay over Medan as well.

Eventually, through the grey cloud and mist, they made out the oil tanks of Belawan Deli, on the coast farther south. It was a fat target, so they abandoned all hope of Pagkalan Brandan and struck this one instead.

They did heavy damage, hitting tanks and shattering pipe-lines running down to the wharves. One Hellcat even managed to find himself a Jap 'Sally' and shot it down.

They were lucky. Not so lucky was a flight of four Corsairs led by Winnie Churchill, the Kiwi firebrand from 1833. Winnie, who had led his flight off half an hour later than the main force, failed to see anything at all through the filmy weather and returned, fierce and frustrated, to *Illustrious*. His lack of success was the more regrettable as he had made history that day by leading the first fighters in the history of Naval Aviation to take off from a carrier's deck loaded with belly tank and two five-hundred-pound bombs. Alas, the bombs only hit safe water when they were jettisoned on the return flight.

But the carriers had not quite finished. Vian gave the enemy a jab as he broke away by throwing a fighter strike at Sabang. Bash Munnoch, the Senior Pilot of 1833, took two flights of Corsairs from *Illustrious*, his own and Don Hadman's from 1830, and strafed their old target for the third time.

It was left for the other carriers of the British Pacific Fleet to strike Pangkalan Brandan a little later, on an occasion when, it was rumoured. Admiral Vian said: '*Illustrious* is too good for that job – we'll let the others do it.'

This operation of Belawan Deli was not a big show, but it was the foretaste of a grim struggle to come. The fierce, impromptu onslaught was the opening move in a long, bitter campaign, which the carriers of the BPF were now to fight and suffer, a bloody eternity of sweat and strikes, strikes and more strikes, against heat and fatigue and the Japanese.

Steve Starkey found a name for it all later on. He called it 'The Thirty Years War'.

On Christmas Day, 1944, Admiral Vian was on board *Illustrious* for morning service. A fighter likes a fighting ship, and Vian seemed to enjoy visiting the Taranto veteran. Then, with the first light of 1945 and a fresh breeze he took his four great carriers to sea. Out in the Indian Ocean he swung them into intensive exercises.

The new British Pacific Fleet was preparing for a great strike against the Japanese in the East Indies. Every attempt was made now to reproduce the conditions of battle.

The attempt succeeded too well for one Corsair pilot. As he came in he missed the wires and slammed his machine into the barrier, covering the deck with flaming oil and petrol.

It was an awful, awesome sight. The entire flight deck of *Illustrious* from side to side and from the barriers aft, was alive with flame. The fierce wind down the deck swept the blazing lake of petrol and oil swiftly farther and farther aft until it seemed that the whole great Ship aft of the crashed plane was ablaze.

Bob Ellison, in attendance as usual on the flight deck, saw the crash in horrible detail:

He saw the Corsair 'float' on landing, miss the arrester wires and smash into the wire barrier faster than an express train, slamming on to its nose and buckling the long-range belly tank which was still partly full. Sparks ignited the leaking petrol. In a few seconds the deck was afire.

Then he saw the frightened young pilot make a fatal and ghastly mistake. Fearing that his whole machine was about to explode, he threw himself out of the cockpit and on to the wing in a frantic attempt to get clear. Instead of jumping off the leading edge of the wing to safety, he leapt from the trailing edge. His foot touched the deck and he slipped and fell in a pool of burning petrol. Scrambling up, he staggered off aft and downwind, away from all the fire-fighting appliances and straight in the path of the fire.

Then Ellison and his party got to him and rushed him to sick bay. The boy had third-degree burns of face neck and forearms, right shoulder, hips and legs. Treatment was begun immediately but with little hope of success.

In the subsequent enquiry, the aircraft was reported as having been, normal before the crash. In fact, all other sections of the report indicated 'normal' – except one vital part, which read:

> 'Goggles and mask not worn during landing-on. Sleeves were rolled up high. Shirt was old, thin and worn. Gloves were worn. Trousers were not tucked into socks and may have been pulled up for coolness. Landing was down-sun. Dark glasses worn.
>
> 'Flying category – A 1 B' (i.e. fully fit for flying duties anywhere in the world). 'Last and recent medical showed no abnormal operational fatigue. nineteen months in Corsairs, twelve of which had been in the tropics.'

Bob thought bitterly how much more he could have done for the boy if the pilot had only obeyed instructions and taken the simple precautions of rolling his sleeves and trousers legs down and fastening his mask and goggles before landing.

Norman and the other Corsairs meanwhile had been ordered back to China Bay. As soon as they landed they were told that the flight deck had now been cleared again and that the ship was ready once more to land them on.

They had the usual long wait for petrol bowsers to refill their tanks, and while they waited, Norman, Reggie Shaw and Eric Rogers lounged together on the grass, Eric and Norman drawing lazily on cigarettes.

'By the way, I don't think I wished you many happy returns,' said Reggie.

'Thanks,' said Norman, 'but make it happy landings, will you?'

'Same thing, boss,' grinned Reg.

'I wonder who that poor kid was who pranged,' said Norman.

'I hope he got out of it all right. Poor old Mike Tritton'll take it hard if anything's happened to him.'

'It certainly looked a terrible shambles,' Eric said.

The conversation flagged. Then a mechanic came over to tell Eric that his machine was ready.

'Well, I'll shove off,' said Eric, 'and I'll have one standing on the bar for you when you get back, boss. So long.'

He walked off, climbed into his Corsair, and in a matter of minutes had taken off. Norman watched him climbing up into the sun.

Reggie went off next, then an 1830 pilot, another from 1833, with Norman last.

It was a lovely late afternoon now. He had five or six minutes to go before he found the carrier, which was still heading into wind away from Ceylon waiting to recover him. It was such a bright, clear, beautiful day, that on an impulse of sheer exuberance he started rolling his Corsair through the empty, endless blue sky. When he got a little farther out, he saw the ship lying down there in the sun, a beautiful sight on the shimmering water.

He levelled out at three thousand feet and approached the ship.

Everything seemed normal, except that when he was about a mile away he noticed a great angry swirl in the water astern of the carrier. It looked like ripples radiating from an underwater explosion, and he wondered whether any of the Avengers had been up dropping depth-charges. He thought nothing more of it, but made his approach and landed-on. Immediately the ship swung round and headed back for Ceylon, all flying finished for the day.

Norman was anxious to know who had been involved in the fiery barrier prang. When his machine was on the for'd lift he jumped out and ran over to the island, leaving a mechanic to take the Corsair down into the hangar.

Up on the compass platform he saw Wings and the Captain anxiously studying a list of names.

'Hans,' said Sarel abruptly, 'who were the ones with you at China Bay just now?'

Norman told him the names. '...Shaw, myself, of course, and Eric Rogers. Why?'

Sarel turned to Captain Lambe.

'It's Rogers,' he said.

Norman stared at him. 'Want a minute,' he said quietly.

'What about him? What's happened?'

'He's just gone in,' said Wings.

'Oh, God,' said Noman. 'Where?'

'Astern of the ship. He was given a wave-off and spun in.'

'That was the swirl I saw in the water, then...'

'Yes.'

There was a long silence. Norman stared foolishly at the list in Sarel's hand.

'You're quite sure it was Eric?'

'Yes. We've accounted for the others.'

' 'I see... What about the other one – the barrier prang? Is he all right?'

'He's badly burned. When I saw him just now he had a cigarette in his mouth. He was trying to make jokes...'

'Thanks,' said Norman, and turned away. *I'll have one standing on the bar for you when you get back, boss.... No, Rog, I'll be buying this one.*

About nine o'clock that evening they were told that the boy who had been burned had died at half-past eight on board the hospital ship. It was with a heavy heart that Norman wrote in , his diary:

> 'Felt absolutely *bloody* tonight – mainly for Rog, such a grand kid.... It was *his* birthday, too – his 23rd – and we were all set for Operation *Bacchus* tonight. Found myself swearing unendingly: overjoyed when Fred (Smallwood, Lieutenant' RNVR, batsman escort carrier *Ameer*) came aboard to spend the evening with us. We were howling, and no mistake; and Rog would have seen eye to eye with that'

They went on with their programme. On the 13th the four carriers did a combined escort and strike practice exercise on Colombo in the morning and followed it up with a fighter sweep exercise over Sigiriya and Trincomalee in the afternoon.

On the 15th the secret was out. All heads of departments were summoned to a general briefing.

'You have no doubt all been wondering,' began Commander (Operations), 'just what the next job is going to be. Well, it's Palembang.'

There was a pause.

'Yes, I know you're none the wiser. Well, I'm going to put you wise. It's in south-east Sumatra and it's the biggest Japanese oil refinery outside

Japan itself. If we can knock it out we shall be doing a good job, particularly for the army in Burma.

'I'm going to hand one or two photographs round. Unfortunately there aren't enough to go right round, but if you can have a look at one it will give you a good idea of how the place will look when you reach it. You'll notice the oil refinery is all on the south side of the river, and that the refinery itself is actually divided by another river running due north to join the other river in Palembang.

'We estimate that it's going to take three attacks to knock the place out. The first attack will be aimed at the main part of the refinery on the west side of the river. The second attack will be on the eastern part of the refinery, and the last one will be a general mopping-up of anything left standing. As usual when attacking oil targets, we want you to hit everything first except the oil storage tanks themselves. If you hit those first you merely obscure the whole of the target area and make it impossible for all the lads behind to see what they are doing.

'Well, there's the general outline of the operation. I shall be holding separate briefing sessions in the next day or so for individual squadrons, according to the jobs.

'The next most important part of the operation is to neutralise the surrounding airfields. This is most important, as Sumatra is the proving ground for all Japanese fighter pilots in this theatre, and with a large number of instructors on hand the opposition is likely to be pretty fierce. In order to neutralise these airfields we are laying on, shortly before the main strike comes in, a fighter sweep from all the carriers. As you know, Mike, you will be leading this and the pilots accompanying you will be notified at later briefing.

'Now, this series of operations isn't going to be easy. It will mean about ninety miles over the water and about a hundred and fifty miles overland before reaching the target, and the opportunities for interception will be absolutely unlimited, so the escort will have to be right on its toes.

'You will all be very relieved to hear that air-sea rescue arrangements are well in hand. We shall have a submarine lying off the east coast of Sumatra, and on the west coast we have established a secret rendezvous for anyone who has to walk home for part of the way. In addition, you will see that on this occasion we have embarked a Walrus. An intrepid aviator by, the name of Walker...' (loud cheers) '...has been cajoled into landing the thing on Lake Ranan immediately after the operation and watching for any pilots who manage to make it on foot.

'We won't go into call-signs and the more intricate details now. This will all be done at individual briefings.

'Well, that's all, except – Mike, Hans, and Charles, I'd like you to stay for a few minutes.'

When the rest of them had gone he gave the three COs their individual briefings:

'Right. Now, on this job, we've got to provide Corsairs for the fighter sweep. Mike, I'd like you to take some of Hans' chaps with you. Hans, I wiant you to release all your ace ground strafers for it. You yourself will be on escort – they're making you low-cover leader. We have to provide only eight aircraft for low cover and another eight for middle cover. I shall leave you to work out for yourselves who you are going to put on, but let me know who you decide on.

'I'd like to see you and your ground strafers, Mike, in the morning about half-past nine, and at about eleven, Hans, we might have a run through the escort drill with your low-cover boys. Incidentally, you will have sixteen aircraft on low cover altogether. The other eight will be Hellcats from *Indomitable*. 'As for you, Charles, I want to see your navigators first of all. I think we'd better make it tomorrow evening after tea, and we'll work out navigation details. The next morning I should like a word with your drivers and air gunners.

'Now, I know that everyone will be wanting a look at this model of the target area. If you let the lads in all at the rush, there won't be any model left in a couple of days, so they'd better be organised to look at the thing in parties. I'll ask the Wing Observer to draw up a rota....'

When he had finished with them, Norman went back into the wardroom. There, Winnie Churchill was doing one of his funnier impersonations. Norman let him finish, then called him over to the bar for a drink.

'Well, boss, what am I doing?' blurted out the Kiwi.

'You're coming with me on low-cover,' said Norman, with a smile.

'Whacko! Suits me!'

'It won't really, you know, Winnie,' said Norman. 'On low-cover you don't get any cowboys and Indians stuff.'

'What do you mean? No chasing 'em down?' said Winnie indignantly, his new beard bristling.

'Not on your life!' said his CO firmly. I once got an awful rocket for leaving low-cover,' he said, thinking of Surabaya and the days of Jumping Joe – how far away it all seemed now! 'No, I'm afraid we shall just have to hang on to the bombers. After all, there's only sixteen of us, and there'll be a helluva lot of Avengers to watch.' He grinned at the crestfallen Winnie, who loved a fight almost as much as he loved the sweet girl he had married back in Cape Town. 'You needn't look so bloody glum about it. If I can believe everything Ops says, there'll be plenty of fun for everybody. In fact, the odds are you'll get more than you bargained for.'

'Roll on the day.' said wild Winnie.

If there was one thing Norman had found out about commanding a squadron by now, it was that you could not *order* a Domimon pilot to do anything – you *suggested* it. Approached the right way, they would go through hell for you – but not if you *told* them to.

'Well, now,' he said casually, 'I think we'd better have a jaw in the morning about this before we see Ops. Then we'll have our plans ready when he talks to us about it.'

'Okay, boss,' said Winnie eagerly. 'We'll get the boys together in the morning. Where do you want to see them?'

'Oh, we'll use the gunroom – give ourselves -room to spread out.'

Next morning in the gunroom he told them what he knew about Palembang and their part in the job.

'We've landed ourselves with low cover again. There are going to be sixteen of us all told, the other eight being Hellcats from *Indom*. Winnie, I think you're the ideal bloke to bring up the rear....'

'Whacko!'

'....I think we'll have the *Indom* chaps on the wings and I'll be up in front.'

'How are we going to arrange the weave on this trip, boss?' asked someone.

'Well, we'll have a matter about it later, but I think we'll be better weaving in sections, using just our own bit of sky – we'd use an awful lot of air weaving in flights. When we reach the point where the bombers deploy, then I think we'll weave as individual flights. The fire power against an enemy attacking should be a lot more devastating that way than if we were just going for him in sections. The order calls for low cover to be five hundred feet above the bombers, and I think that's just about right – we must have room to manoeuvre if things get dicey. Now, has anybody got any ideas?'

'There is one thing; boss. We always have a helluva time while the Avengers are getting up to the altitude. I'm always miserable hanging on my prop.'

'Well, the answer to that one is – get going faster! It means doing a lot more weaving and using up a lot more gas, but if you don't mind the weaving, I don't mind the gas. We'll have loads to spare with the belly tanks, even if we do have to drop them fairly quickly. Any more questions?'

'Are we going down with the bombers at the far end, sir?'

'I'll make up my mind on that when we get there. We don't know an awful lot about the defences. We've never mentioned balloons, but there's always that possibility. We don't know what the ack-ack is like and, of course, we don't know what the fighter will amount to. If there are balloons and the ack-ack is pretty hot, there's no point in our going down with the bombers. We should be doing a much better job by hanging around up aloft holding off the fighters and waiting until the bombers appear again.

'Is there anything else anybody wants to know? If there isn't, there's just one thing I want to say. The odds are that the fighter opposition may be pretty hot, even allowing for the sweep which is going in beforehand, and it's an absolute *must* that you should all be smack on the ball and looking after each other as much as ever you can. I don't want anybody coming back saying, "I don't know what happened to him, sir, I never saw him go," and above all – leave the R/T alone as much as you can. Use it only when one of the fighters is in real danger of being jumped, and whatever you do don't waste R/T space warning the Avengers of fighters. They've got enough to think about and it's our job to look after them without bothering them.

'Now, this afternoon I've arranged for us to have a look at the model. It won't tell us much, except the ack-ack positions, but at least it'll give us one or two ideas as to where we will re-form with the Avengers, and also where we ourselves can rejoin if we get scattered. We'll have another meeting later on this week when we'll go over this again and get radio call-signs fixed. Okay.'

So proceeded the long, complicated pattern of briefing, sandwiched, as always, between the eternal exercises. On the 17th the Corsairs were up, on the following day the Avengers. On the 19th, as the day scheduled for the great strike drew near, the fighters stood by all day on deck. But on the 20th the weather broke down and continued to blow a gale throughout the next day.

On the 22nd, the day planned for the operation, waves were crashing down on the flight deck. At night the force turned about and went back. On the 23rd, however, the weather improved, and they tried again.

On January 24th, 1945, they did the job.

They took off, one after another, from the four carriers forty-three Avengers and sixty fighters to escort them. Then the Corsairs of the fighter sweep shot off the deck, and went on ahead of the main force.

Bombers and escorts reached enemy coast without incident and went roaring steadily on across the jungle at twelve thousand feet, fighters weaving, heavy-laden bombers rising and falling slowly like a fleet at sea.

Norman, at the head of his escorting fighters, realised they were getting near when the Avengers opened the taps and his Corsairs and Hellcats had to stoke their own fires. Then he saw the hazy outline of the Malacca Straits opening-out ahead like a great highway to the heart at Japanese power. Then...

The Avengers suddenly began to open out to deploy for bombing. There was the refinery below them – just like the map – and a dirty green fungus with red spots rising slowly and malignantly up to meet them. Balloons!

The R/T started.

'Rats nine o'clock up!'

One or two tiny specks were hurtling down through top cover, whistling down like bombs from something like thirty thousand feet.

Ack-ack burst around them like a rattle of tin cans. The fighters shuddered and reared, weaving in flights together now, looking for trouble.

A Jap flashed in from the port beam, with one or two of middle cover behind him. Norman wheeled his whole flight to port and they opened up. He broke downwards, away from the shattering punch of the .5's.

Now there were Tojos and Oscars all around them, coming in singly, in unco-ordinated attacks.

An Oscar flashed across Norman's mirror, firing wildly, then dived. A moment later he surfaced in front of them, climbing. With one accord the Corsair pilots heaved back on their sticks and gave him the devastating broadside of twenty-four .5 machine-guns.

They saw an aileron flutter off, then a gun panel from the wing. A hole blew out in the fuselage and he rolled off in a stall.

Another came in from the port side. Norman watched him. Then, from his number two... look out, Hans! Bandit to starboard!'

The flight wheeled to starboard and opened up from dead ahead. The Jap fell, burning, incendiaries bouncing off his engine cowling, and passed beneath them with only a few feet to spare.

Then Norman realised that Reggie Shaw was not with them. *I'm sorry, sir, I didn't see him go.*

The Avengers were well into the attack by now. The balloons were up, and Jap fighters were swarming, so the Corsairs and Hellcats stayed aloft. Skirting the balloons, they rejoined the bombers on the other side of the target.

Going round the north-west side of the refinery, they were astonished to see a twin-engined Jap fighter form up with them to starboard.

With a look of alarm he broke away. The Corsairs hastened him on with a quick burst which rattled up his port wing and set the port engine on fire. He went over on his back and spiralled down into the blazing ruin of the refinery.

The strike was done, or rather the first part of it. Now there began the long, dangerous run home, leaving one Avenger in the deadly web of the balloons. Fending off further attacks by Jap fighters, they made for the coast.

Then the sea was below them once more, friendly and smiling now, a shining pathway to the ship.

Another Avenger broke down.

'Sorry, chaps, my elastic's come unwound,' was all they heard before the bomber ditched.

At last – there was *Illustrious*. Wearily they orbited waiting to land.

This was the time when deck landing took its toll, now, when a pilot was weary and his reflexes played ragged like sagging bowstrings.

Slowly, so slowly, the Corsairs came in one by one to land, like great tired birds sinking down on the warm earth of a sunny land after an ocean crossing.

Norman watched, aching and weary, as each one turned in over the run-down, lurched to the deck, stopped dead, then crawled forward like a huge wasp on to the lift and was swallowed up in the warm body of the sbip.

Then it was his turn. He put his wheels and hook down as he flew down the starboard side of the ship. When he was well ahead, he tumed to port and went round on to the down-wind leg at five hundred feet.

Halfway down he started putting his flaps down. It was then that he realised something was wrong. Full flap – and still no loss of speed....He must have been hit.

He juggled with the controls, fighting the speed down to ninety knots. By now he had lost a lot of height and was well past the stern – too late for a safe turn to the deck.

Wtth eighty-five knots on the clock, he found himself well astern of the ship on the port quarter, at about two hundred feet. He turned in to port and approached the stern.

There wasn't much chance of seeing the deck. He was still a long way away, with the Corsair's great nose obscuring the view. Normally he would have come in off the turn, with the batsman and the deck well in view, but be had been forced to leave it too late.

He increased height as he approached the ship.

Bats was signalling 'Roger!' and he settled down for a long let-down on to the deck.

Suddenly the ship vanished – blotted out by the heavy shape of a Corsair ahead of him, cutting in sharply off the turn.

His Corsair was almost stalling and the slip-stream from the other machine helped to finish the job.

Quickly he opened up to full throttle, to lift on his flaps out of trouble. But he stalled before he could make it. The Corsair plunged to port in an incipient spin, lurching on to its port wing towards the sea, now frighteningly close.

The aileron was jammed in a tight stall. He fought with both hands and his left knee to move the stick, but could not budge it.

...The sea raced in at him... he screamed with the fear of ugly, jarring death, all the time, instinctively, fighting harder to bring the plane out...

The Corsair picked up flying speed. Controls centralised, he started to pull her, ever so gently, out of the dive.

He held his breath. The sea was very close. His nerves were screeching – but he could hear the engine clearer now.

'I've made it!' he thought.

Then there was a great, blinding crash.... The world went black and he knew no more.

He came to – and found he was drowning.

It was dark and choking, and he was hanging upside down in his harness.

Hitting out with his left hand for the hood, he found he was amongst the control levers of the engine. Gasping and choking, he fumbled with outstretched hand above his head and struck the Perspex.

There was a narrow opening between the hood and the windscreen. Somehow he ripped his harness off and dragged himself out through the gap. Looking up, he saw the lighter green water near the surface.

He gave a violent jerk to get free and reach that wonderful light so near. ...But he was held fast by his parachute. So he had to push himself back into the cockpit, undo the junction box, rip his helmet off, and start again.

This time he made it and rose up through the water towards the surface, half-drowned, gagging and swallowing water.

As he rose he remembered to blow up his mae west with the carbon dioxide bottle. He could see his Corsair lying vertically in the water, nose down. When he broke surface he saw that there were about three inches of rudder showing.

Illustrious had gone. All he could see afloat was his belly tank, which had broken off with the impact. It was about fifteen yards away and would have made a good lifebuoy, but he did not have the energy to reach it. All he could do was to lie back in the water, gasping for breath and choking with salt water every time a wave swamped him. He saw a smoke-float which *Illustrious* had dropped, burning very efficiently three hundred yards away.

By now all initiative, an feeling had gone. He lay there numb, without thought or energy even to, get lid of the revolver and ammunition and the machete which they all carried against the event of a jungle crash, or to pull off his heavy shoes. He even forgot the sharks.

For about twenty minutes he lay there. Then, to his unspeakable delight, he saw a destroyer. The ship tore in from the north and hove-to about a hundred yards away. He could not stand the agony of waiting as he, watched a whaler slowly descend from the davits and start to pull away in his direction. With a tremendous effort he made himself look the other way.

He was almost unconscious, but he remembered being dragged out of the water by hands pulling at his mae west. Then he passed out.

'The poor bostard's had it,' said the cox'n of the whaler as the boat pulled back to the ship.

The pilot lay on the bottom of the boat like a dead fish.

They took him aboard and along to the doctor. The destroyer, the *Wessex*, was at action stations, and the doctor was at his post in the wardroom, with his surgery laid out around him. He and his sick berth attendants stripped the pilots sodden overalls from his body and wrapped him in a blanket.

Norman regarded them, hardly able to see, and totally incapable of speech.

'I'm hanged if I know what to do with you,' said the doctor, 'but I don't think this will do you any harm.'

Thankfully the pilot gulped down a tumblerful of neat whisky.

The doctor bandaged a big gash on his knee, which had been bleeding heavily, and bathed a great lump which had come up on the back of his head where the edge of the cockpit hood had struck him and knocked him out.

For the next hour and a half Norman did nothing, except fed unspeakably ill, and retch up huge quantities of sea water every time his head fell forward, the salt water gushing in great, cascades from mouth and nostrils.

At lunchtime, however, he was very much better, apart from general woolliness and a terrible headache. By the afternoon he had recovered sufficiently to be able to go on to the bridge and do aircraft recognition for the Captain.

Next morning *Illustrious* came up and the following signals passed between the two ships:

'TO: WESSEX   FROM: ILLUSTRIOUS

Intend recovering HANSON today, weather permitting.

(1) Lower a boat ahead of me and I will stop and pick him up.

(2) Scrambling net suspended from my starboard crane.

(3) Scrambling net from my starboard quarter.

Which do you prefer?'

TO: ILLUSTRIOUS   FROM: WESSEX

Your 0828.

I would prefer choice 2.

Scrambling net suspended frool starboard crane.'

Later that morning *Wessex* went alongside the carrier and Norman made ready to leave, inflating his mac west to maximum and shivering as he waited.

There must have been upwards of thirteen or fourteen hundred men lining *Illustrious* starboard side that morning, waiting for the free show to begin. The carrier's crane swung over the narrow gap between the sheer sides of the two ships, lowering the scrambling net, which had been rigged on a boom. Lashed, to it were three sacks of bread – Norman's ransom.

The destroyer men wrenched off the loaves, but the net was jerked away before he had a chance to grab it. On the next run, however, he managed to clutch it and was immediately whirled off the deck of the destroyer before he could get his feet on to the rungs of the net.

A moment later he made his smoothest-ever deck landing aboard *Illustrious*.

He went below to his cabin, and there be found something which touched him deeply.

On the table was a glass full to the brim with neat rum. Propped up against it was a little card reading simply:

'Jolly good luck. sir.
May you *always* come back.'

It was a gift from the squadron ratings, and he felt it more than anything else he could remember since he had joined the Service.

He was under medical care for some time, and while be lay idle in his bunk he learned the rest of the aftermath of Palembang.

Two Avengers from the other carrier had been lost, together with four of *Illustrious'* Corsairs and their pilots. Bud Sutton had gone, from 1830, and 'Tiddles' Brown, with whom Norman, had joined *Illustrious* from Macrihanish on that bleak December day so long ago. Evan Baxter from 1833, too. had been lost and Reggie Shaw.

Norman tried to get news of Reggie and eventually one of the Avenger observers told him he had seen Reggie's Corsair hurling to the ground with two Jap fighters on his tail.

Poor Reg, he thought, and remembered that afternoon at China Bay when the three of them, he, Eric and Reggie, had sprawled on the grass in the sun and talked. Half an hour later Eric was dead, and now he himself had almost gone the same way. And Reggie... and little Baxter.... and Bud Sutton... and eleven others from the Fleet.... For the first time he thought: God! Where will it stop?'

He found little consolation in the coldd fact that those who were lost had helped to make Palembang an outstanding success. But it *had* been a success. The bombers had destroyed their objective, and had wiped out half of the main source of Japanese aviation spirit. A large part of the great refinery lay in charred ruins, and the fighters had destroyed about fifty Japanese planes.

Sixteen against fifty. 'I suppose it's a good score,' thought Norman, as he slowly gathered together Reggie's things – his uniforms, the limp khakis and the stiff blues with their single gold band and bright wings, a pack of cards, a pair of dice, a photograph... the same every time... all to be packed into cases, sewn up in canvas and returned, leaving the cabin empty and meaningless, and a small part of *Illustrious* gone for ever....

Bob Ellison had already had experience of pilots who seemed to have foreknowledge of their own death, and it was during the Palembang operation that he met it again. A young pilot with whom he was particularly friendly crossed the wardroom and asked him to have a drink.

'Well, cheers. Doc!' he said. 'I'm afraid this is the last one we shall have together.'

He showed no sign of nerves or fatigue, and when Ellison suggested that he should ground him, said:

'Thanks, Doc, but it's not a bit of good. My time's come and that's all there is to it.'

The following day he flew his already burning Corsair in through the doors of a Japanese hangar. Another boy, a little later, was discovered to have brought his diary up to date and to have left his effects in order so as to cause the minimum trouble after his death.

Another part of the aftermath of the first great Palembang raid was that they must go back now and do it again, to finish the job as planned and destroy the remaining half of the target, to wipe Palembang refinery off the map:

'Sunday, January 28th, 1945 (day before 2nd Palembang op.).

'Going like a train all day, heading for Sumatra. If the weather is fit, we attack

Palembang again tomorrow. Willie (McGregor, Surgeon-Commander, RNVR, PMO) says I am still groggy after being concussed and have NOT to fly tomorrow.'

For the second strike the pattern was very much the same.

At 0700 Mike Tritton led a fighter attack on the airfields, which was followed by an Avenger strike on the remaining part of the refinery. The bombers hit their target once more and Palembang was finished. At 1000 the striking force returned. *Illustrious* had lost two Avengers, those of Armstrong and Charlie Mainprice, the CO. No fighters were lost from the ship in action, but 1830 low three in bad prangs on the return trip. Results were summarised in a Press communiqué which stated:

'Photographs show that many of the principal installations received direct hits and were afterwards burnt by oil fire from adjacent oil reservoirs. During the attack, aircraft at 3,000 feet were shaken by a particularly violent explosion.

'Fighter opposition was on a reduced scale, as the enemy had been unable to replace the losses inflicted during the previous visit. Seven enemy aircraft were found and shot down over the target area, with three probables. Four were destroyed on the ground.

'Six of our aircraft were lost to the enemy.'

A Japanese radio transmission made after the second raid was reminiscent of other Axis efforts in Europe:

'Total of ninety enemy planes including seventeen probably shot down by Nippon interceptors and ground batteries when some 130 carrier-based aircraft attempted to raid Palembang oil installations..... Damage suffered to our oil installations negligible. Yesterday's war result brings total enemy planes shot down in his two recent attempted raids on Palembang area to 203 planes, not including thirty-three probables.'

There was one difference this time. Some Japanese aircraft penetrated the combat air patrol over the Fleet and attacked our ships.

Bob Ellison stood on the fight deck and watched one Japanese plane which had escaped our Seafires and Hellcats flying down the port side of the ship. He made out a light winking from the aircrafts rear cockpit.

'What's that silly bastard trying to signal us for?' he said to Colin Cunningham, the senior batsman, who was standing nearby.

He realised his mistake almost before he had started to speak, and was wondering how he could possibly have confused the wrong end of a turret cannon with an Aldis lamp, when the whole deck shook under him with the terrifying WHAM! WHAM! at shells exploding inboard.

They were, six-inch shells and they had come from one of our own ships, which had been too zealous in firing at the Jap plane, It was a tragic accident of war, and no one regretted it more bitterly than the gunners who had fired the fatal shells.

Bob Ellison had to wipe a dead man's spattered blood and brain tissue from his eyes before he could see to attend to the many casualties that lay scattered over the flight deck. For some he could do nothing, for others just a battle dose of morphia and a label. The main difficulty was to locate them all, treat them and fix priority labels and yet at the same time arrange to be where he could readily be found. As he was about to shift one badly wounded petty officer down to the transfusion and operating theatres, the man suddenly spoke and said, 'No, sir, shift him first, he's worse than me.'

On the following day *Illustrious* oiled from a tanker at sea. The 31st found her going hard for Fremantle. For Palembang had been done on the way to a newer, vaster battleground farther east. At last the British Pacific Fleet was going where it belonged – to the Pacific.

Admiral Fraser had gone ahead of them in the *Howe*. One of the first things he did on arrival in the Pacific was to go to Pearl Harbour for a conference with Fleet-Admiral Nimitz, Commander-in-Chief Pacific Fleet and Pacific Ocean Areas. The situation as regards the British Fleet was complicated. First, there was the problem of supplying the ships. The resources of Australia were devoted to General MacArthur's forces and to the American Admiral Kinkaid's Seventh Fleet. Even the airfields which would be convenient for the use of the British carrier planes were under American control. However, Admiral Nimitz directed Captain C Julian Wheeler, USN, the first senior US naval officer to be attached to the British Pacific Fleet, to tell Admiral Fraser that 'we will make it work regardless of anything'. In any case the American forces were now about to move out of Australia in the wake of MacArthur's advance. The real problem would begin when the Royal Navy had to supply a fleet operating over four thousand miles to the north of its nearest base. Unlike the US Navy, we had had no experience of operating a Fleet Train of supply ships.

On February 6th, Norman had a medical check-up. He came out of it fairly well, but could only manage to hold the mercury column steady for thirty seconds.

'Is this the best you can do?' said Ellison dubiously.

'Lets have another shot,' said Norman.

It still wasn't a very good performance, but he added ten seconds this time.

'Oh, well,' said Bob, 'if you want to fly I suppose that'll do.'

He actually flew again on the 9th. *Illustrious* had arrived off Sydney and the Corsairs went ashore to Nowra airfield south of the town. Then the ship put into Sydney to have some surgical attention herself.

Her centre, and main propeller had been damaged during the Palembang period, so she went into dry-dock to have the screw removed and repaired. Some of the sternmost frames of the ship had also suffered damage, and Commander (E) Bud Newsom was kept very busy.

Throughout February repairs went on aboard the ship and her planes ashore did a lot of flying. On the 12th, Norman, who had lost Corsair 690 in his crash after Palembang, flew his old and favourite Hunter FT 371, 'Kathleen III', up to Bankstown, where he turned her in for a new machine. 'She's been a grand bus, bless her,' he wrote in his diary. Back at Nowra he recorded several hours as pilot and passenger on various different Corsairs, Tiger Moths and Avengers, and on the 24th he went to Jervis Bay to do ADDL's, with an abortive attempt at some more four days later. He wrote: 'Went with Percy Cole to do ADDL's at Jervis Bay, but the wind was all to hell and Johnny Hastings waved us away. Bags of gas but no maps! So decided to explore. By dint of retentive memories, instinct or something, we flew across about ninety miles of saltpan country and hit Canberra right on the nose! Had a look at the local Westminster, a long – and close! – goof at some lovelies in an open-air bathing pool, and rounded off with a highly illicit, but very enjoyable, beat-up of the local RAAF fighter airfield. Waited all night petrified lest the phone ring, but apparently *this* time nobody has objected!'

In these blue and friendly skies, in the luxury of sweet air and sunshine, the pilots flew and skylarked. Australia sprawled, luxurious and lazy, like a big, brassy, indulgent blonde, beneath them and it was on her infinitely friendly and maternal bosom that they relaxed and took their pleasure, a little desperately, when they came down from the white purity of the clouds. This treasure hunt for the golden hour was pressed with greater and greater urgency as the future sidled stealthily closer. Tomorrow – reality. They ate, drank and were exceedingly merry.

And if the pace was hot – just around the corner was 'Operation *Iceberg*'.

Okinawa is an emotion in American hearts. It is a name for genius and greatest courage, for the terror and agony of men, for some of the bloodiest, bitterest fighting of the war. It was a campaign in which all parts of amphibious war were active, from the most savage hand-to-hand combat on land to great fleet actions at sea, a campaign of ancient savagery and new weapons, of iron defence and desperate assault, of wave against rock. And in the end Okinawa was a name for glory.

In all this our sailors had a part, and a proud part.

'Operation *Iceberg*' was the code name for the great assault. At advanced bases all over the Pacific a vast force of US Navy, Marine Corps and Army awaited its call to action, backed by the huge mobile complex of logistics, whose floating and flying lines of supply and reinforcements stretched two thousand miles across the wide blue expanses of the Pacific, like living arteries from the great throbbing heart of America.

Part of this amphibious juggernaut was Task Force 57 – the British Pacific Fleet. Under the overall command of Admiral Bruce Fraser, it would be led at sea by his second-in-command, Vice-Admiral Rawlings, with Vian, as Rear-Admiral, Aircraft Carriers, exercising tactical command whenever air operations were in progress. Task Force 57 was really part of Admiral Spruance's Fifth Fleet, as the first numeral of its designation denoted, a companion of Admiral Marc Mitscher's famous Task Force 58, though numerically smaller. As such they would be serving under a great sailor – Spruance, the victor of Midway and of the Philippine Sea, a man modest in manner, but probably the greatest fighting admiral since Nelson, a man who, as a great American historian has said, 'simply went on winning battles for his country', without gas or glamour.

The British Pacific Fleet was going to be there to play a vital role in helping him win this battle.

Their job, as part of Task Force 57, was to dam up one vital channel of Japanese reinforcement to Okinawa from the west.

From China to Okinawa was a chain of stepping-stones formed by Formosa and the Sakishima Islands. On every stepping-stone the Japanese had built airfields. When the attack on Okinawa began they would try to fly in planes along this chain of airfields.

The British carrier fliers had to stop them.

It would mean a constant, relentless pounding of airstrips and a combing, night and day, of the air above them, to keep the net drawn tight and take some of the pressure off the US Army and Marines on the bloody beaches farther east. It would be grim – and probably costly. The ack-ack defences were bound to be formidable, and resistance more vicious than they had ever met before. This was where they were going now, up to a front line of fire in the north-west Pacific.... 'How many of us will come down again?'

On March 7th it began. The planes left Nowra and flew aboard *Illustrious*. Then the great ship turned north and headed for Bali H'ai – and the stark reality beyond.

The miles of glittering sea unfolded, me deceitful, smiling waters that held so many broken ships from the earlier Pacific battles:

'Sunday, March 11th, 1945.

'Today, about noon, we entered the Jemard Passage, between the Louisiade Archipelago and the island reef of New Guinea. The scenery is wonderful; the islands vary from massive out-crops of rock to green, flat reefs with lovely golden sands. Just like a fairy tale.

'In the Solomon Sea tonight.'

On the way up to fhe fronfthey flew whenever they could and practised the things they were likely to nwd when they started-operating:

'Monday, March 12th, 1945.

'.,. experimented with breeches buoy with *Undaunted* and *Urannia*....'

On the 13th they reached Manus. They stayed based beiefor a few days, exercising at sea in heavy rainstorms and drinking at the *'O' Club* ashore. Then, on the 18th, the four carriers left and crossed the Equator at eight o'clock that night. On the 20th they entered Ulithi lagoon, a great, smooth stretch of blue water enclosed by a rough, rocky atolls. There, at Ulithi, on the 22nd, there was a general briefing aboard *Indomitable*, the flagship of Admiral Vian.

On the 23rd, the first assault on Okinawa began.

The British ships left Ulithi at 0700... 'the pride of the King's Navee', wrote Norman. 'Shouldn't think we've had such a fleet since Jutland – or maybe Trafalgar – *Indom*, *Indefat*, *Vic* and ourselves (modesty!); *King George V* and *Howe*; *Euryalus*, *Black Prince*, *Gambia*, *Argonaut* and *Swiftsure*; *Grenville*, *Quality*, *Quiberon*, *Quickmatch*, *Undine*, *Undaunted*, *Wager*, *Wessex* (God bless her!!), *Queensborough*, *Ulster*, *Urania*, *Kampenfelt*, *Whelp* and *Wakeful*.

At sea the fighters got their eye in with some air-to-air firing at drogues towed by American Marauders.

On the 26th they took station one hundred miles to the south of the Sakishimas, and their part of '*Iceberg*' began. Log-book recorded,

'Strike on Sakishima Gunto: airfields.'

For the first time they flung themselves down from the eye of the bright sun upon those criss-cross runways, deadly with thick ack-ack – and came back several pilots and aircrew short, Runway were blasted out of action, aircraft shot-up on the ground.

Next day they went to Ishigaki, the boot-shaped island with the fiercest flak of all – the flak that got Nottingham, CC of *Illustrious*' Avengers, and his crew.

Now the pattern was – strike and rest, strike and rest... on and on in a hazy chain of hard action and relentless reaction, with losses mounting and pilots, observers and air gunners getting steadily more and more weary and 'twitched'...

'...bags of flying all day. Wrote a few letters tonight, *Bloody* tired...'

...so that every deck landing, sometimes with a shot-up aircraft, became a thing of jumping nerves and quaking guts....

'...*ginormous* barrier prang today. Bill Christie, 1830...'

...that repented itself again and again until nerves could take no more and another pilot wrote himself off and perhaps an observer and gunner as well.

Strike and rest, strike and rest... 'Fighter sweep over Ishigaki' ...'Top cover to strike on Myako and Ishigaki'...

Strike and rest... strike and rest... strike and rest... with no end. The strikes were all the same, beating up planes and gunners on the ground, filling airstrips with bomb holes so that at night the Japanese could fill in the holes and fly in more planes ...for Avengers and Corsairs to blast and strafe again next day, leaving behind them, inevitably, a shattered Avenger, a burning Hellcat or Corsair, like marker flares for the next maximum effort of nerves and brains and tired bodies....

In all this strain and struggle there was one source of strength which never failed. When the tired, sometimes wounded pilots returned from another hard strike on the gun-sewn rock of Ishigaki or Myako, they knew that she was there and would always be there as long as the battle lasted – *Illustrious*, that great and wonderful lady they all loved and needed so much, familiar, maternal, restful, her great deck a steadfast refuge, her cabins and passages like the well-known well-loved rooms and corridors of home. You saw her familiar shape below you breaking the hard glitter of the sea, and you thought, for the umpteenth time, 'There she is. God bless her, steady as a rock, just as men had thought at Taranto and Salerno and Madagascar before you. You got down, and there was Bob Ellison with a fag for your nerves and a patience and friendliness that never failed to soothe. There was Wings and Arthur Wallis and the Captain, and the rest of the boys in the wardroom. There was your cabin, where you could relax and write out some of your tension in a letter home. And later, in the wardroom, there was old Hans at the piano, with a big smile, as usual, on a dog-tired face, and Mike, who would die rather than let you know his real feelings, bless the stiff-necked old bastard... the ship, thank God for the ship.

Two or three days of strikes, the pattern was, then a lull, when Task Force 57 pulled away exhausted and spent two days, two blessed, peaceful days, resting and replenishing, leaving the escort carriers of Admiral

Blandy's Support Force to relieve them on station.

The carriers were really moving airfields now, switching their daily strikes from island to island in this long artery to Okinawa, unable, however, to remain on station permanently. Fuel ran out, and food; bombs, bullets and planes were expended; morale ran low, too, and tired pilots wanted a word from home, a letter written weeks before in Cape Town or Carlisle, in Vancouver or Warramunga, in Sussex or Saskatoon.

All these they got from the ships of the Fleet Train, by the grace of the great god Logistics. The huge floating commissariat at the Fleet Train itself lay at an advanced base. When battle-weary ships withdrew from station, a Logistic Support Group would be detached from the main body of the Fleet Train to meet them at sea.

Tankers, supply ships and repair and replenishment escort carriers met the British Task Force a few hours steaming away from their battle station, and refreshed hungry and thirsty ships, planes and men in the open sea. *Almost* everything was catered for, except, as Bob Ellison said, '...unfortunately, popsies, plenty of beer, fresh milk and vegetables...' There was beer of a sort, but not the real McCoy. It was the weak American beer and came, in Ellison's phrase, 'in things like brasso tins'. But at least there was the flight deck beer garden, a creation of Captain Lambe's, where the ratings could drink their bottle at Sundown every evening. It was a fantastic sight to watch, out on the open sea, a carrier 'plugged in' to a tanker on one side, sucking in oil and aviation spirit through dangling hoses, with a destroyer passing her sacks oft mail and another ship fuelling on the other side of the tanker – 'Like a sow with a litter at piglets,' wrote Ellison.

During one of these welcome lulls Bob was invited to a party in the warrant officers' mess one night, where a very congenial celebration was being held for some of the officers of a destroyer which was tied up alongside. There was one particularly pleasant bearded lieutenant who joined in with great gusto and was especially interested in some of the uninhibited songs that were sung that night. When be returned to his ship, his host, the Chief Shipwright of *Illustrious*, asked Bob if he had recognised their bearded guest – Prince Philip of Greece.

Too soon the holiday came to an end. Tanks were topped up, bellies were fat again and nerves were almost, though never quite, mended. Then the whole weary, dangerous business started all over again, with the gunners on Ishigaki and its brothers getting better all the time, and casualties mounting in the squadrons. Day after day the battle of attrition wore on. 'Combat Air Patrol – Sakishima,... 'CAP and Scramble' ...'Fleet Train' ...CAP and Strafe – Myako' ...'CAP and Strafe – Formosa: NE coast'

...'Close escort leader – Strike on Shinchiku, N Formosa. Scramble and CAP'... 'Fleet Train'.

Strike and rest, strike and rest ...and then, the pattern changed, and there was a new word for tear – Kamikaze!

The word itself meant 'Divine Wind' and was supposed to refer to the great storm which smashed four thousand Mongol ships coming to invade Japan in June, 1281. But the pilots who were part of the new Divine Wind thought of themselves as members of *Tokubetsu Kogekitai*, or 'Tokko', the 'Special Attack Force' organised by Vice-Admiral Takijiro Ohnishi in October 1944, to combat the mounting force of the American offensive, then directed against the Philippines. The specific target of that first attack force of First Air Fleet had been to render the American carriers ineffective for at least one week. 'In my opinion,' said Admiral Ohnishi, 'this can be accomplished only by crash-diving on the carrier flight decks with Zero fighters carrying 250 kg. bombs.'

Ohnishi could advance this opinion in the full confidence that his young pilots would accept its implications without question. The centre of Kamikaze was morale, and they were completely disciplined in the old Japanese military tradition which taught that an act of self-immolation for the greater glory of the Emperor was the supreme honour. 'The cherry is the first among flowers, as the warrior is first among men,' ran the saying. Now, each young Japanese warrior-pilot was given the choice, 'Living, to be overwhelmed with the immeasurable blessings of Imperial goodness; dead, to become one of the Guarding Deities of the country and as such to receive unique honours in the temple.'

As each man flew out to die he had this ancient code to stiffen his purpose. Perhaps he would think of the words of the Emperor Meiji, which had been written up in gold letters above the gate of his first military training barracks.

'Remember that death is lighter than a feather, but duty a heavier than a mountain.'

From Leyte onwards Kamikaze was a major weapon,used deliberately by the Japanese High Command to beat off the US Fleet and avert the worst consequences of the war. They took, in all, two thousand five hundred young men, all ready and willing to die for the Emperor, and hurled them upon the American Fleet, using up their large reserve of obsolescent planes for the purpose. They knew that, although the American, anti-aircraft barrage and fighters were deadly against normal attacks, the American carriers with their wooden flight decks were 'soft tops'. Carriers severely damaged would have to retire to Pearl Harbour, seven thousand miles away, and would be out of the war for some three months, thus severely damaging land operations. Japan had everything to gain by these tactics and nothing to lose, for the death of two thousand men was 'lighter than a feather' compared with the possibility of making the United States so war weary that Japan might be able to negotiate for peace without further loss of face.

It was a logical move, in the light of Japanese history and military tradition. But it failed, though causing grievous damage and loss of life to American ships.

At half-past seven on the morning of April-fool's-day, 1945, a Divine Wind hit the British Pacific Fleet for the first time when a Zero dived straight on to the bridge island of the carrier *Indefatigable*. There was some damage, and several casualties were sustained. But the British carriers were not 'soft tops'. They carried three inches of armour plating on their flight decks. To the utter surprise of the Americans, *Indefatigable* was operating her aircraft again in the afternoon.

Meanwhile the destroyer *Ulster* had taken a Kamikazi right through her iron deck and into her boiler room. Then a 'Deadly Johnson', as the British matelots called them, went in very fine off *Victorious*' bows.

Five days later it was the turn of *Illustrious*. The gunners saw him coming, diving towards the forward part of the ship.

Perhaps he was following the usual Tokko practice of aiming for the forward lift. Whatever he had in mind the Bofors gunners changed it for him, knocking him about so much that he exploded over the side.

But he left some souvenirs behind. The starboard wing of the suicider had actually crashed into the bridge about nine feet away from Captain Lambe, and pieces of plane and pilot were scattered over the flight deck.

Bob Ellison bent down rather dazedly and picked up two eyeballs and a piece of skull. He was looking stupidly at them when Don Hadman, a wild Kiwi from 1833, dashed up and grabbed the piece of skull from his hand.

'Thats my mascot from now on!' he yelled.

Then he booted the eyeballs over the side, for Don had never heard of the Emperor Meiji and cared even less for the immeasurable blessings of Imperial Goodness. Even so, he very soon helped yet another young acolyte towards deification and 'everlasting honours in the temple?, for Don was carrying his mascot when he took off and stopped the breath of the next Divine Wind to appear over the Fleet.

The strain was ailing on everybody sow, and not the least upon the ship's batsmen. The two of them, Cunningham and Johnny Hastings, slaved from early morning until late at night at their difficult and highly responsible job. Mentally they shared each cockpit, made every approach to the deck, their nerves pitching and falling in tune with the pilot's own anxiety and fear of pranging in flames or drowning in a sinking plane.

On one particular day Johnny Hastings 'batted on' sixty-one aircraft. It was not surprising if these two highly skilled, hard-working and conscientious men suffered as much from battle fatigue as the pilots. The Deck Landing Control Officer seldom received the credit he was due for this absolutely vital job – a job which did not end with the responsibility for the safe landing and take-off of the ship's aircraft, for the planes had always to be correctly and efficiency arranged on deck, and that was a headaching part of their job too. Before every take-off, fighters and bombers had to be properly 'spotted' aft, dovetailed neatly together so that, no confusion resulted when a strike subsequently left the deck. And when the planes returned and were eventually brought on to the deck, there was the additional headache, and backache, of arranging the deck park. *Illustrious* kept a permanent deck park for'd of fourteen aircraft, for which there was no room in the hangar. These had to be spotted and made secure. With the advent of the Divine Wind and the possibility of a Kamikaze crashing into these planes, all the fuel had to be drained from their tanks each night. This hard chore kept the squadron ratings, the aircraft handling party and the Deck Landing Control Officers hard at it until neatly midnight – and got most of them up again at half-past three the next morning.

And if it was difficult and deadly tiring on deck, it was uncomfortable enough below. A pilot going to his plane when the ship was in the tropics dare not touch the metal, baked almost red-hot by the fierce sun, with his bare hands, but between decks it was, if anything, even worse. As Ellison wrote:

> 'In crowded bathrooms men would be "dhoheying" their battledess overalls in the little fresh water available; others would be on watch in machinery spaces at very high temperatures; in the galleys, sweating cooks would be preparing action meals in the shape of sausage rolls and Cornish pasties to be eaten by men at action stations, while in the hangar, as in a light-tight tin box, men stripped to the waist were making final adjustments to the aircraft; and all this with the tropical sun beating down so hard on the steel deck and ship's sides that you could not bear your hand on the inner surfaces.'

Bob himself was getting a bit 'twitched' by now. He had lost too many good friends, he had watched too many deck landings with his heart in his mouth, his nerves strung up to... 'Christ! Will he make it?...'

He watched the strain overtake them all, and only the toughest, and the luckiest, survive.

He saw Don Hadman, returning alone and badly shot-up, fired on by our own gunners in mistake for a Kamikaze, and Percy Cole's flight almost go the same way. A Seafire, coming through the clouds on the tail of a 'Deadly Johnson', was hit by the barrage intended for the Jap and shattered to bits.

More happily, he saw Bud Newsom apply the toe of his boot to the pants of a Pay Sub-Lieutenant who had been disputing 'the ownership of a deck-chair with a weary lad just back from a strike. What put added fury into the kick was that the Commander, who hardly got any sleep at all himself, had just given up the chair a moment before to the tired pilot.

He saw Jimmy James, of 1833, crash. Jimmy stalled when coming in to land and dived steeply into the sea from a hundred and fifty feet. His cockpit hood was blown off on hitting the water and he himself concussed for a few seconds. Luckily, Jimmy had his wits about him and was cool enough to release himself when he came-to under water. He rose to the surface and, was picked up by a destroyer. The accident report ran:

> '"Q" type harness undoubtedly minimised injuries, and all other encumbrances had been undone on coming in to land. Body completely covered. Injuries – concussion (mild); comminuted fracture of elbow, dislocation of head of radius and bruising of left hip and thigh. Face and head untouched. Previous recent category A 1 B.
>
> 'Pilot had been airborne operationally twelve out of previous 36 hours *but was otherwise not under any strain....*'

He saw another young sub-lieutenant come in, miss the arrester wires, bounce over the barriers and nearly go down the for'd lift, hit a crane with his wingtip and crash into the sea in flames off the starboard bow. He was rescued alive from the wreck, but the shock produced immediate symptoms of thyrotoxicosis, so that after a few hours his eyes protruded abnormally and his thyroid gland began to swell. These and other symptoms, including tremors of the fingers, got him sent back to base via the Fleet Train when the carrier pulled out of the firing line.

He watched the gradual disintegration of Percy Cole, the perfect pilot, whom every young pilot aboard had been urged to emulate for the smoothness of his deck landings. Percy was an example of the way in which the best sort of British, as opposed to Dominion, pilot degenerated from operational efficiency under these appalling conditions of strain and fatigue. A British pilot tended to do so slowly, perfectly conscious of and prepared to admit his own degeneration from full efficiency but simply soldiering on until he had to be grounded.

Ellison worried over Percy's case, as he did over them all. As fatigue set in, Cole's landings became more and more ragged until he simply threw his Corsair at the deck and hoped for the best. In the air, and in combat, he was still as able as ever, but the approach to *Illustrious'* deck found out his battle-weariness. Gone was the old certainty that be would catch the third or fourth arrester wire. It was obviously only a question of time before he piled up seriously.

The expected happened. He came in, missed all the wires and crashed amidships. Stepping out of the shattered plane unhurt, he reported to the bridge.

For heaven's sake, Percy, what happened?'said Sarel.

'I just forgot to cut the throttle, sir,' said Cole. I'm sorry.'

And it wasn't so very long before he did the same again. This time his aircraft, missing the wires again, slammed to the deck and screamed on its nose straight for the island, scattering fight deck personnel right and left; scoring a long screeching track with its twisted airscrew.

Again Cole climbed out unhurt. It was once too often for Bob Ellison. Percy was grounded.

Normally the Flight Deck Medical Officer's grounding order overruled all others, but Cole, Senior Pilot of 1830, was irreplaceable, and Wings insisted that he must fly again.

'Surely you're not going to send him up again, are you, sir?' said Ellison.

'I've got no replacement for him,' said Sarel. I've *got* to send him up again.

So Percy went back to Ishigaki and Myako and Formosa and gave the gunners lining the scarred airstrips a little more practice, while Bob continued to do what he could for his friends, watching them go out, fighting the battle of their fatigue for them, wondering who would be missmg this time, watching each approach as the Corsairs orbited on return, his own nerves jumping as each one plunged to the deck, having a word with each man as he ducked into the island out of the fierce wind that tore down the deck, always ready with a fag and that unflagging sympathy which they all knew and unconsciously relied upon.

The fighter boys he felt to be his special charge. Roy Aldridge looked after the Avenger crews, and between them the two doctors did all they could to keep morale high and perhaps, they hoped, helped to save a life from the twin devils of Ishigaki and the deck.

Norman Hanson would often come to Bob's cabin and let off steam, talking himself through his worries to a clear mind again. Mike Tritton, more reserved, never let himself speak directly about any personal strain or worry, but kept to squadron matters or painted glowing word pictures of Eton, which he obviously adored. His only sop to superstition was the can of beer and tin-opener he always carried tied to his belt when he flew, 'If I bale out on Jap territory I shall at least have one consolation,' he used to say.

Both these young squadron commanders had the DSC, both were 'Temporary' officers. All through this terrible period of attrition they continued to lead their squadrons, and Mike the whole Wing, with great coolness and care. They were just as tired as the men they led, much wearier, in fact, with the greater weight of responsibility resting upon their shoulders, just as aware that it was only a question of time before they, too, bought it. But their cheerful leadership never faltered. The doctor watched them all get slowly more and more tired, more and more unsure of their passes at the deck. The Dominion boys were rather different from the British in this respect. With them, there was as a rule no long period of slow degeneration from full flying efficiency. They would continue at more or less full efficiency up to a point when they would suddenly crack, so that the doctors might have as little as twenty-four hours' warning.

On April 7th, Winnie Churchill took a flight to Ishigaki.

'No more than two runs on the airfield now, Winnie!' warned Norman. "Those bastards are hot. If you do a third run they'll get you.'

Winnie said nothing,

'Yes, I know what you're thinking,' said Norman, 'but just remember the kids with you.'

They went to Ishigaki and made their two runs. On the way back Winnie suddenly signalled that his radio had gone out of action. This meant that he must automatically pass the leadership of the flight over to someone else. When he saw that all was in order, Winnie broke away, turned – and went back to Ishigaki. On Saturday, Norman wrote sadly in his diary:

'Our dear old Winnie killed this evening by the devils on Ishigaki. A gun in the town got young Marrit. Rugged day.'

On April 11th, Norman led a three-hour patrol off Formosa in very bad weather. Every entry in his diary now finished 'Tired' at 'Very tired'.

The next day they went back again, led by the Commander (Flying) of *Indomitable*, and struck at Formosan airfields, destroying a large number of Jap planes for the price of one Avenger and two Corsairs, Norman narrowly escaped being shot down when his wings were perforated by flak and his Corsair flung over on its back. That night he wrote to Kathleen:

'...Poor Jake Millard was lost today – you remember him at Stretton: the trig, bluff, cheery cove in Mike's squadron. He was with me on an escort job this morning, in shocking weather, founding the northern end of Formosa. Suddenly he piped up to say that his engine was fading and asked to be allowed to turn back. I had to let him go, though we were a long way from the Fleet. Just after he turned and disappeared. I decided to send Johnny Baker to keep an eye on him. Johnny, good kid, came up with his usual Toronto "Wilco, boss" and turned back too. He caught up with Jake just as he ditched, about four miles off the coast. Johnny promptly banged out the "May-day" to the Fleet, who whistled up a US Navy flying boat. They've been searching all day, until dusk tonight, but no luck.

'Poor Johnny feels it badly, but he has no cause to criticise himself. He had to climb way up above Jake to get R/T contact with the Fleet. When he went down he could not find Jake – a man's head with a mae west collar takes some finding in the north-west Pacific. Jake's a damn good swimmer and may have made Formosa. But, even so, I don't fancy his chances. The characters who live around there are none too pleasant. Mike is upset tonight – we all are, for that matter and we're still stunned at the loss of our one and only Winnie and young Marrit last Saturday. Jack Parli, Winnie's pal from years back, is a man in a dream, and I feel for him...'

On the 13th there were two more strikes on Formosa. By now nothing Japanese was to be seen in the sky over their aerodromes. There was nothing visible intact on the ground, and the Corsairs were going down to ground level looking for hidden aircraft.

The Avengers, too, had to grind on, filling the same old airstrips with craters lest the Japanese should stage in planes from China at night.

On the 14th *Illustrious* joined the Logistic Support Force once more. That morning somebody stuck his bead round Ellison's door and shouted:

'Wakey, wakey! – Get up and took what's on the starboard bow!'

It was *Formidable*, fresh out from England – their relief on the battle station.

After that they simply shut up shop and went home, and left the war to somebody else.

CHAPTER TEN

THIS WAS *ILLUSTRIOUS*

Coming home was a light-headed feeling. Everything was totally unreal. *Illustrious* was a strange ship. All the way from Aussie they followed a lazy track, with all the sea-birds doing hornpipes in the air. It was lazing and loafing all the time, sunbathing and smiling all over your face for no particular reason at all.

No more flying. The aircraft had been dumped ashore at Sydney. If they ever went to Tokyo somebody else would be flying them. And if their former owners would not be in at the kill – *Hell! Who cares! We've done our job.*

As they steamed through the Bismarck Strains between land still held by the Japanese which no one thought it worth while now to mop up, the end of the war in Europe was announced.

Illustrious celebrated with a *feu de joie.*

It was a double celebration for them, of course, and they needed no encouragement. Guns that once snarled at Kamikazes now went off in all directions like fireworks. The ship spliced the mainbrace and Nelson's Blood ran in rivers. Bob Ellison never knew who put him to bed that night. All he could remember was staggering around with a Bren, scattering tracer like golden rain, with David Mahoney, the Captain of

Marines, making unsteady attempts to see that he did not kill anybody.

There was a sequel to this explosion of joy. In the cold and unfunny light of dawn Tokyo Radio announced gravely that amphibious forces of the British Pacific Fleet had attacked the Japanese-held Bismarck Archipelago and had been repulsed with heavy losses. The news really set the seal on their homecoming, and after that even sillier things happened.

Where the Pratt and Whitneys had roared such a short time ago there was a different song to be heard now. They lugged the long-differing wardroom piano up into the hangar and trundled it on to the lift. Up from the depths like a cinema organist rose Norman Hanson, playing 'Three Pilots We' to the accompaniment of massed cheers and whistles. There were many of these flight deck concerts, with everybody bawling themselves hoarse

In the middle of the Mediterranean, Captain Lambe hove to and piped 'Hands to bathe'. It was the best swim they had ever had. There may have been some very good naval reason for calling at Gibraltar, but the main aim seemed to be to lay in large stocks of sherry and other goodies to take back with them.

Then they were home. Slowly *Illustrious* made her way up the Firth of Forth to Rosyth, her paying-off penant trailing proudly and sadly right aft, and all the ships on either hand hooting and cheering a welcome. Only the utterly insensitive were able to keep full control of their emotions.

They left *Illustrious*, eager for leave, and most of them never saw her again. It was only later that they thought much about the old ship and dug deep into their memories in an attempt to bring to life those days of struggle and comradeship the like of which they never found again.

But there was one man who went back to her soon afterwards. Norman Hanson, like everybody else, rushed home from the ship. He spent much of his foreign service leave in Carlisle. Here he relaxed and enjoyed himself, but as time wore on he began to get restless and preoccupied. Then he thought of *Illustrious*. It wasn't really far to Rosyth, and he thought Kathleen and his father would like to see 'The Ship'. He wanted to go for some other reason too, a vague, unsatisfied longing to see the old lady again and settle something, he scarcely knew what, for himself.

As the Queensferry boat took them across the Forth he could see clearly the fighting top of his beloved *Illustrious*, towering up from the Lilliputian tangle of lesser ships' masts and funnels. He was unmistakably bright-eyed and eager, and his heart beat faster as he jolted the car through the dockyard and towards the dry-dock where she lay.

And there she was – shored up by timbers, blotchy and chipped, thickly barnacled below the water-line, unnatural and ungainly out of her element, shabby and sorry.

The dockyard mateys were in possession aboard and there was only a small staff left. Quickly he showed his wife and father round the ship, then John Smallwood entertained them to tea.

During the after-tea chatter he escaped. For the last time, he felt, he must look round alone, with his thoughts to himself.

He climbed from the wardroom flat to the after starboard lobby, then into the hangar.

Empty. The steel walls echoed and rang as he walked slowly through it, hands in pockets. *This was our pitch. That's where the lads pranged Gordon's elevators into the bulkhead*. He left the hangar by the for'd port lobby and went up to the flight deck.

Empty. Cold. Lifeless. A cigarette packet blowing across the deck by the barriers.

Up on Wings' bridge he leaned down and stared the length of the flight deck. It wasn't real. This wasn't *Illustrious*, this wasn't the old ship. This was a steel hulk, cold and inanimate.

And then the thought of the life that had once been in the ship. He pictured a crowd of pilots down below – Winnie, dear old Winnie, left behind many thousands of miles away on Ishigaki, ragging Colin Cunningham, and getting verbal hell in return; Bud Newson weaving his skilful way to a goal at deck hockey; Reggie Shaw being helped from his Corsair in the crash barriers, young Eric taking off that last time into the sun....

But they weren't there. None of them would ever be there again. Johnny had been right, too right – they *hadn't* all come home. But even those who had returned were no longer '*Illustrious*'. The four winds had caught their wings and scattered them.

Then, suddenly, as he stared, the memories came rushing back dizzily, calling and clamouring with a single voice, and he understood....

Illustrious wasn't this poor, deserted, lonely shell, dumped in a dry-dock. She wasn't even that majestic lady along whose stately flank he had flown so often.

She was and always had been – always must be – that happy band of men who had lived and worked together, played, fought and died as one soul – the soul of this great ship. '*Illustrious*' meant the rumble of the Avengers as they taxied up the deck, the scream of an arrester wire as a Corsair streaked in for a landing, the songs around the piano, the game of darts on the squadron's mess deck.... But always it meant *people*. It was the men who made the ship. For some, *'Illustrious'* had been Denis Boyd, Williamson, Going and their contemporaries – for him, Bob Cunliffe, Charles Lambe, Ian Sarel, Arthur Wallis – and all their eighteen hundred officers and men. These he would always remember, long after the outline of the ship had become blurred in his mind.

He went ashore a happy man.